SIX YEARS AT UNITED

ALEX
FERGUSON

6
YEARS
AT
UNITED

BY ALEX FERGUSON
WITH DAVID MEEK

MAINSTREAM
PUBLISHING

EDINBURGH AND LONDON

First published in Great Britain in 1992 by
MAINSTREAM PUBLISHING COMPANY
(EDINBURGH) LTD
7 Albany Street
Edinburgh EH1 3UG

ISBN 1 85158 444 7

A catalogue record for this book is available from the
British Library

Typeset in Ehrhardt by Alphaset Graphics, Edinburgh
Printed in Great Britain by Butler & Tanner Ltd, Frome

For Cathy and our three sons.

CONTENTS

Chapter One

CLIMB EVERY MOUNTAIN

We know we threw the Championship away last season but the bitter disappointment has made us only more determined than ever to go out and show everyone we are the best team in the country. People are saying we will never get a better chance to win that elusive League title and I confess that my immediate reaction last April was to feel that we had let down the fans who so desperately want the championship trophy at Old Trafford. But all that is behind us now. We are raring to go again. The players are ready for it and so am I. We have stopped feeling sorry for ourselves and, for sure, we can face another challenge. God works in mysterious ways. Maybe it was the final lesson for us, the ultimate experience in humility and a reminder to our younger players of how it feels to have victory snatched away at the moment it seems in your grasp.

The important thing is that we must not allow ourselves to think that Manchester United's failure to win the League title since 1967 is some kind of curse on the club. We must not sink into a slough of despondency, believing that the world is against us, because that way lies defeat and the possibility of submission. If you give in once, you will always give in and I assure you that that is the last thing that is going to happen to this club. Perhaps the players riding high on a couple of years' success will better appreciate victory when it comes. Their bitter failure could make them better men and players of distinction. It might just be the final lesson as we work towards creating a team in the fullest meaning of the word.

Certainly, we must not be paranoid about last season's final débacle in terms of the Championship because it was, in fact, a good season. The club is in good order, with talented young players coming through and I have strengthened the squad. I shall remind everyone of our successes last year. We won the Rumbelows League Cup for the first time in the club's history and we won the Super Cup. We won the FA Youth Cup and we went damned close to winning the League.

I try to analyse every season and naturally I had to take a good hard look at what went wrong . There is always a danger of too much analysis, too many statistics, too many pointers, but nonetheless you have to examine in order to learn. Firstly, I had to ask myself whether I was prepared to start all over again and I'm happy to say that it never crossed my mind that finishing second would be my final challenge at Old Trafford. Sir Matt Busby was 58 before he won the European Cup. He had a few disappointments along the way, indeed tragedy when his fine young Busby Babes were destroyed at Munich, but he never gave up. I am still only 50, a fit 50 though I say it myself, and if I need any inspiration I just have to look at the career of the Grand Old Man of British football.

The final few weeks drained me, no question about that, they drained my wife Cathy and our house was like a morgue. She said she didn't know whether she could go through it all again but we talked that one through and from now on she's going to let me do the worrying. We have simply got to get away from thinking: 'Hell, we'll never get a better chance'. I remember an old friend from Aberdeen saying to me after we had finished second in my first full year: 'Aye, maybe that's the best you'll ever do. You've got a tough job at Old Trafford.' Well, we came out of that trough and last season we got ourselves into a marvellously challenging position with a set of good young players.

I looked at the highly rated Dutch national team at the 1992 European Championships and was amazed at the number of players they had around the age of 29. I was reminded that coming up to 30 is a peaking age for players. We have a few players like that but they are well backed up by lads in their early twenties like Gary Pallister and Denis Irwin who are both 25, Paul Ince who is 24 and

Andrei Kanchelskis at 22. Peter Schmeichel is 28 but that's young for a goalkeeper. Then we have youngsters like Lee Sharpe and Ryan Giggs thrusting forward with a flock of even younger players on the horizon from our successful youth team.

The composition of our squad is right and what we have to do is dismiss the assumption that we will never have a better chance. It's nonsense. Who says we won't? The big advantage we have now is that when we next get ourselves into a challenging position then we shall be able to draw on the experience of last season. Even for me, there were certain things I had never experienced before and which shocked me. I'll be better prepared now. I will be better able to cope with the contradictions of football. For instance, how can you explain Nottingham Forest working so hard in the key League game against us, harder than they did in the Rumbelows Cup final, when there was obviously so much more at stake for them? Hopefully, I will be better fitted to understand West Ham's unbelievable display against us. Even their own manager was at a loss for words to explain their outstanding performance. He even apologised to me after the game. He was embarrassed that his team had played like Dervishes after being relegated.

There is a certain envy for Manchester United which surfaced at the wrong time for us and made our task all that much more difficult. We know about that kind of thing now. I won't be as shocked if I hear a repeat of the Liverpool player who shouted from the dressing-room: 'F*** you'. I learnt something that day, something I had not come across despite being a manager for some 18 years.

I have won plenty of things in my time and I have lost big games as well but I have never come across the situation we had in the closing few weeks when our failure seemed to make a lot of people happy. I don't want people to weep crocodile tears for us but I find it difficult to understand why rivals should take so much satisfaction from someone's downfall. It's bitter and twisted but we will be ready for it next time. In fact we can use it to our advantage this season. It will be a cause for us, a rallying point to make sure we try even harder.

Perhaps I shall be reminded that after winning the European Cup Winners' Cup I came boldly out to say we would be going for the Championship. Some thought I was over-ambitious and had left myself open to be shot down but I take nothing back. Maybe we tripped over the last few hurdles but we had a good season. We were front-runners with Leeds for nearly all the campaign and the first thing I did at the end was to congratulate Howard Wilkinson on their success. Then I sat down with the staff to talk about the young players and the marvellous season they had had, reaching two finals in international tournaments in Switzerland and Germany and, of course, winning the FA Youth Cup. I was so proud of them and I am delighted with the progress we have made in that area. I want to maintain that operation because I think it is so important.

Right from the start of the season I fancied our boys to win the youth competition and they delivered some unbelievably good performances. I spoke with David Pleat at Luton after our game there in April and he said he couldn't believe the quality of our side. He said his scout had told him to watch out for Tottenham and he had been surprised to read that we had beaten them 3-0 in the first leg of the semi-final. Then he had noted that Ryan Giggs had scored two of the goals and Spurs had had a man sent off so he thought that Giggs had done it on his own.

He went to the second leg in London himself and told me he couldn't credit how far ahead we were. He reckoned that we have conquered the youth scene in England for the next five years with the young players we've got. What people outside Manchester don't, perhaps, appreciate is that Giggs played in relatively few of the youth ties because of his commitments with the first team. It is in fact, a great side even without him.

Incidentally, Tottenham had seven boys in the England youth team, yet we won the Cup with not a single representative. Talk about Southern bias – though I believe the FA took the view that our boys were mostly first-year trainees and, as such, they did not consider them. That is no excuse for not selecting Simon Davies. He made so much progress last year and was captain for most of the time when Giggs was not available.

Spurs were very highly rated and we were worried about the wet conditions for the first leg at Old Trafford. They had a stronger side in the sense that they were mostly second-year boys, but our lads handled them well and by half-time had a two-goal lead. We won 3-1 with two goals from Ryan Giggs and an own-goal. Obviously with a lead like that we were confident about the outcome in London and, in fact, won the second leg as well with goals from Nicky Butt and Ben Thornley giving us a 2-1 victory.

So we qualified for a final against Crystal Palace where the concern was again centred on the strength of our opponents who were a particularly big, physical side. However, we went to London and came home with a splendid 3-1 win, Butt scoring twice and David Beckham getting the other. The return leg fell as we were trying to get over the disappointment of missing out on the championship and the outcome was a soothing consolation. We had a super 15,000 crowd to see the boys on a lovely sunny evening – not so sunny, I might add, when Palace scored in the very first minute. The youngsters recovered their composure and scored through Ben Thornley, Colin McKee and Simon Davies for a 3-2 win on the night and a satisfying 6-3 aggregate success which is an impressive result by anyone's standards. Some of the football played by our boys was a delight.

The successful squad was: Pilkington, O'Kane, Switzer, Casper, Neville, Beckham, Butt, Davies, Giggs, McKee, Thornley, Savage, Burke.

There are five or six who will certainly go to the highest level, an exceptionally high ratio from any youth team. As always, we try to look for flaws and reasons why we can be wrong but, frankly, we don't see any. Time will tell, of course, but in my view all of them will make the grade in professional football and, at a conservative estimate, I believe five are capable of reaching the standard necessary to play in United's first team. This would be a marvellous achievement, with shades of the Busby Babes and the team of 1964 which last won the FA Youth Cup at Old Trafford and went on to supply that star-studded era of George Best.

It was a terrific end to the season. It was great to see the youngsters' faces and the obvious enjoyment of the supporters when they lifted the trophy. I'm not suggesting that the FA Youth Cup can replace the League Championship but it was still very heartening to find the lads succeeding in such a brilliant fashion to give us a real boost for the future.

Manchester United are a good football club again with players from seniors to juniors who care for the club. There is a real degree of passion and commitment and there is a good standard of skill. So the answer to the question of whether we can pick ourselves up to make another serious challenge for the Championship is a wholehearted yes. The players themselves want the challenge above anything else. They desperately want to prove themselves. Of course other teams, especially Leeds, the reigning Champions, will have similar ambitions. That's great because it gives us the makings of a good competition.

People went on last season about how it was a two-horse race in an inferior league. Strangely, they never said anything like that when Liverpool were winning the title by a dozen points or so. To my mind that's when you could have said it was a poor competition because there was no-one in sight to challenge, just one dominating club. At least Manchester United and Leeds had a tremendous battle, with other clubs not too far away, and I believe we will see an even more competitive tussle this season. The English First Division, or Premier League as I suppose I must describe it now, is not easy to win. We had lost only two League games right up until the latter part of the season and didn't win. That tells you just how much consistency is required to become Champions.

The players are keen to go all the way this time. We have still got the best support in football to help us. I know there are worries for the fans, like prices and a shrinking Old Trafford, but I know they will still be there for us as a source of inspiration. We have waited a lot of years to win the League. No-one knows for sure whether it will be this season but I do know we will have a right go at it.

One experiences a lot of disappointments in life, especially football, because it's in the nature of the game, indeed it's what the whole of sport is all about – that there are winners and losers. Normally, you ride through defeat because you know there is another time. Now and again, though, comes a set-back which doesn't just numb you for a short while but hits you straight between the eyes and leaves a vacuum in your life, a void which at the time seems inescapable. You wonder how on earth you are going to get out of it and how long it will take to repair the damage.

I have been down that road twice, once as a player and then as manager of Manchester United after seeing the Championship snatched out of our grasp. I know how our support must have felt going into work on the Monday morning after losing at Liverpool, of all places. They had my sympathy and I felt desperately that I had let them all down. I wrote in the programme after one match at Queens Park Rangers that I had wanted to shake everyone by the hand for their quite marvellous response. Now I wish I had because the encouragement given to us throughout the season was unbelievable.

But this summer I have had to make a determined effort to rid us of this guilt feeling because it would have been destructive to wallow in that kind of misery. I have tried to take a positive line, seeking ways of rising again. My message to our supporters is that we won't let them down again. The traditions built by Sir Matt Busby will not be allowed to waste.

I said when I was appointed manager at Old Trafford that I regarded it as the pinnacle of my career. There are still mountains to climb but we are all in the mood to climb them. And to help us I went into the transfer market to sign 23-year-old Dion Dublin from Cambridge United for £1 million. If we had scored a few more goals in the latter half of last season we would have won the Championship. Our scoring slipped badly and we needed a shake-up with the stimulus of a new face. Dion Dublin has a good scoring record and will add to our arsenal. He will provide some interesting alternatives because he is different from our other strikers. At 6ft 2in he has obvious power in the air, but we have studied his scoring and his goals show a good variety because he also has a neat touch for a big man. We will see how he settles before I decide how best to use him. I was certainly delighted to sign him because the deeper we got into negotiations for Alan Shearer, the less I liked the vibes. Dion is very positive about his transfer and I am sure he will be a success – as well as perhaps helping to boost our scoring rate.

Chapter Two

THE LEGEND

Only through success can a manager become master of his own destiny.

Success unlocks all the doors. Set against a background of two or three trophies, decisions can be made with a ring of conviction, players accept what you are saying without doubting, supporters sustain their belief through the inevitable set-backs and you become a figure of authority without the need to look over your shoulder. Success achieves all these things as well as giving a manager security at home, knowing his job is safe.

I feel these things are happening for me as manager of Manchester United. It's one of the reasons why I feel able to write this book and record my six years at the helm of Old Trafford.

But I assure you that this sense of belonging at the club has only come after many sleepless nights and painstaking work. As I say, it needed some success for all the parts to fit. It certainly hasn't always been like this. No manager can really be prepared for the job at Old Trafford. The legend is huge. It's so different from any other club in Britain.

I knew all about the record of Manchester United when I decided to quit Aberdeen and take up the challenge of Old Trafford. I knew it was a club laced with traditions and great expectations. That's why I was prepared to turn my back on Aberdeen and the security I had gained there after winning ten major honours in eight years. I had a great understanding with the old Chairman at Pittodrie, Dick Donald, and I had a very nice lifestyle without too many worries.

It was a great feeling when Aberdeen peaked under my management, and particularly when we captured the European Cup Winners' Cup. What a climax that was when we beat Real Madrid in the final in Gothenburg, 2-1 in extra-time.

In my time there I turned down chances to manage Rangers, Arsenal and Spurs, but when the opportunity came to join Manchester United I could no longer stay in my safe house in Aberdeen. I felt I had not achieved enough, and once you stop striving in football it's time to chuck it all in. So I was ready, and it didn't take long for me to reach agreement with Martin Edwards.

But although as I say, I knew all about the history of Manchester United and was fascinated by the prospect of taking charge there, I had no real inkling about the demands. I repeat, no manager is prepared for the job at Old Trafford. The directors and supporters are so lucky because they haven't been at other clubs. I think it took me three or four years to understand fully the politics and requirements, the demands and pressures. For the first time in my life I felt my whole character and abilities were under scrutiny and that I was in a situation where my future would be decided not only by directors of the club, but also by supporters and the media.

I would get to the ground and see two directors talking, and there would be a fleeting moment when I would wonder what they were talking about. It's amazing how it can transmit itself to become guilt – you feel you are with this great club and wish you could give them something that tells them what you are about.

There are periods when you are trying to achieve things but it is not recognisable. I am talking about the organisation of the club within, the youth scouting and coaching, the training patterns and the behaviour of the players. It was something that was never going to be quickly appreciated or understood, because the thing that really matters at our club is the winning of matches and doing so with a style and panache that has made people so proud to support us.

Eventually you become part of it yourself and you are linked with this obsession to give the supporters what they want. You want it so badly yourself. Some of our supporters are happy to see us lose, provided we score four goals and entertain them. I have had letters saying how much they appreciated a match we have lost, that they have enjoyed the performance, and that is something which is unique among supporters in the land.

Football affects their social life so much in Manchester. It's as if their whole week is crammed into 90 minutes of a Saturday afternoon or a Wednesday night. I felt for the fans after we had lost 5-1 to Manchester City, for instance. What could they say when they went into work on a Monday morning – or did they go in?

I watched Glasgow Rangers as a young boy and I know myself what it is like going into a factory after your team has lost. I know as a player as well. I remember the Monday after being relegated with St Johnstone and there was this tradesman, a lovely lad, but he had a wee go about Second Division wages the next season. You expect sympathy when you have been relegated but shop-floor humour is not like that. I gave him a mouthful. So I can understand what our people went through after we had lost 5-1 at Maine Road.

Our support is unique. How else can you explain the consistent size of our crowds when we have not won the League Championship for 25 years? I remember soon after coming down from Aberdeen saying at a press conference that I hoped it would not be another 25 years without the title, and I set myself to win the League just as soon as I possibly could. I am well aware that some good managers before me have failed, but I am not prepared to think along negative lines.

When I first arrived Manchester United seemed a mystery to me. To an outsider it's difficult to understand how a club which didn't win the League could attract such a big following. It was a mystery I wanted to become a part of, though. In Scotland you are never quite so close to a club, but because of Sir Matt Busby every Scot feels he is a second cousin or is related in some way. He is so much loved and respected by Scottish people, and at the same time he is an inspiration.

The Scots have always been travellers. They look at people like Carnegie in America and Busby in England and feel that with a bit of luck they could end up like them. This is especially true in football because every Scot is born a player and they have this great love for the game. It's what makes so many of them 'tanner ball' players. We like to show the world how good we are. It's in our make-up, and if I am honest, it is part of the lure which brought me to Old Trafford.

The Scots have a wee inferiority complex which makes them all want to do a bit on the football pitch. They are great individualists, perhaps too much so, because when it comes to playing in a World Cup the Scotland teams have never done particularly well.

When we are in a crowd there is a swank and cockiness about the Scots, but we are never to be underestimated because it is usually accompanied by a fierce determination to succeed, whatever the obstacles. Sir Matt Busby had this quality. His early days in England were not particularly successful, but he was determined to succeed as a footballer and he did before becoming one of the great managers of all time. Bill Shankly was another with this extraordinary will to win and become a success at what he did. Perhaps it's a quality which has been useful following in the footsteps of Sir Matt who, according to many pundits, cast a shadow over his successors.

I can honestly say I have never felt inhibited by his success at Old Trafford. I had heard what I regarded as rubbish and thought, why should this be? I was proud to be going to a club with a great tradition, and it was a tradition built by Sir Matt. Quite frankly, there are very few clubs with this kind of tradition, so I felt lucky rather than intimidated.

I don't see history as an obstacle at all. Indeed I wish Sir Matt had been younger so that I could have drawn more knowledge out of him. He has always been helpful to me and he is helpful to everyone.

I believe that any manager who has tried to say he was inhibited by the shadow of Sir Matt was making an excuse, except perhaps for Wilf McGuinness, who was so young and inexperienced when he was asked to take over. There was a kind of father-son thing about that appointment. No other manager could possibly say his job was made more difficult by interference from Sir Matt.

So I certainly did not have any hang-ups about a Busby shadow when I decided to break away from my comfortable life in Aberdeen to step into the unknown with Manchester United.

It was obvious United were having a difficult time. Their low League position told you that, though it is not for me to examine Ron Atkinson's management. Everyone is different and you simply cannot say who is right and wrong. For instance you won't find a manager with a more contrasting style compared with me than Brian Clough. He doesn't even train his team, but he was in the final of the Rumbelows Cup against us and he has had more than his share of trophies in a long career with Nottingham Forest, so he must be doing something right!

All I wanted to do was assess the present and look at the future against a yardstick of knowing that we had to win the Championship as quickly as possible, and that that would be the yardstick against which I would be judged.

The team were languishing near the foot of the table, second bottom in fact. My first game after taking over was on 8 November 1986, at Oxford, four days after the team had gone out of the League Cup, losing a replay at Southampton 4-1.

We lost 2-0 and the team I inherited lined up: Turner, Duxbury, Albiston, Moran, McGrath, Hogg, Blackmore, Moses, Stapleton, Davenport, Barnes. Sub: Olsen. We drew at Norwich the following week, and then came home to Old Trafford for my first win with my new team, beating Queens Park Rangers 1-0 with a goal from John Sivebaek.

All teams respond to a new manager because judgements are being made, and we made a little progress with only two more matches lost in the following three months. But it didn't last, with five games lost in the final 12, and we finished 11th in the table.

But I had had time to assess the situation and I had not liked what I had seen. When I met the directors at the end of my first half-season I told them we needed nine new players to win the Championship.

To put it mildly, I think they were surprised. I think they felt that all that was needed was a fresh hand on the tiller, but what concerned me was the fact that there were too many players on the wrong side of 28 or thereabouts. They were too old to go for the challenges I had in mind. Individually, they all still had a lot of football left in them, but collectively they added up to a team which, while experienced, had lost the magic spark.

There was Gordon Strachan, Frank Stapleton, Mike Duxbury, Remi Moses, Mark Higgins, Gary Bailey, Kevin Moran, Arthur Albiston and Peter Barnes. There is no harm in having a couple of 30-plus players, as we have now, but there were too many, with not enough 26-year-olds coming up and in turn not enough youngsters pushing them. You have got to have a mix.

I looked at all the contracts, ages and the number of games certain players had missed with injury and wondered how long some of them would last. It was a case of simple arithmetic. I had to be hard-headed.

I suppose Frank Stapleton was the biggest disappointment. Here was a much respected player holding a record number of FA Cup winners' medals, two with Arsenal and two with Manchester United. His reputation was as long as your arm, but he had lost his mobility and he just didn't look as if he would ever score a goal. I had a problem, though, because he had not signed a contract and the situation was tending to unsettle everybody.

I was new and I wanted to get the spirit right so I reached an agreement with him. It was a mistake. Frank was introverted and bordering on the morose. He certainly didn't smile a lot and as one of the players said when I eventually sold him to Ajax: 'Perhaps we can all laugh a bit now.' He was certainly a shock to me, a shadow of his former self, and in fact I started to feel sorry for him. It was sad.

I also inherited a few long-term injuries. Gary Bailey had damaged his knee the previous season, and though he went to the World Cup in 1986 he only aggravated the damage and he was eventually forced to quit.

Remi Moses was another player I was sorry to lose. He had a bad ankle, but was a brilliant little player. Quiet and shy off the field, he didn't mix much with the other players, but in action he was non-stop and a great talker, with a good knowledge of the game. His passing was particularly good, always carefully made at the right angle away from markers and delivered with the exact weight.

His excellent tackling was abundantly clear to everyone, and but for his bad ankle I am sure he would still be playing today, because he looked after his body and fitness. He was probably underrated generally, but not by me. I don't think he played more than a dozen games for me before he was compelled to retire. I have hardly heard from him since. I met him once and asked him to come down and perhaps do a little light training with us, but he just keeps away. I don't know why, because he would always be welcome.

But though I was worried that we hadn't got enough young players to accept the challenges I had in mind, there was not a lot of money available to spend in the transfer market. I think Ron Atkinson had been given his head the year before and had spent quite a few bob on the likes of Colin Gibson, Peter Davenport, Terry Gibson and John Sivebaek.

I felt I was left with trying to make a silk purse out of a sow's ear. At the same time I was adjusting myself to a few things like the relatively luxurious life of the players compared with my frugal days in Aberdeen where we never travelled with more than 14 players, and who had always had to pay for their own phone calls and newspapers when we were away from home.

I have always been a believer in a firm upbringing for young players, even a stickler for some things, like insisting on a blazer and flannels for certain public appearances. Eric Harrison, who was here when I arrived, is the right person to be our youth coach. He doesn't give them an easy ride. There are certain things we do for the young players which are important, like providing a dining facility at the training ground to make sure we put the right fuel into their engines. That's an important luxury which I think we do well in the process of producing young athletes. You also want to instil a self-discipline in your youngsters, or at least a willingness to accept discipline. If they can't there is no future for them.

One of the things that shocked me in the early days was the poor standard of the youth side and the reserves. It meant I had to look at the whole set-up involving our scouting and recruitment of young players, and my verdict was that we had got it wrong. I took over a system which had 20 scouts in Scotland, yet in Greater Manchester, with a population almost the same size as Scotland, we had only four – Harry McShane in Manchester, one in Bolton, one in Rochdale and Joe Brown operating as our youth development officer.

It was simply out of balance and there was plenty of criticism of the club flying around – rightly so, too. Manchester City were in front in this area and it had shown the previous April when they beat us in the final of the FA Youth Cup. City had a whole stack of promising lads emerging like David White, Steve Redmond, Ian Brightwell, Paul Simpson, Paul Moulden, Paul Lake and Andy Hinchcliffe.

From that 1986 youth team we produced only Gary Walsh and Lee Martin for our senior side. It goes in cycles of course, because four years earlier our youth team sported Mark Hughes, Norman Whiteside, Clayton Blackmore, Billy Garton and Graeme Hogg, a good clutch who all made it. There was no doubt, though, that when I arrived we had slipped. I immediately set about doing something because I have always prided myself on producing youngsters and I had done well at both St Mirren and Aberdeen.

I have always considered that the player you produce is better than the one you buy. There are loads of exceptions of course, but it's a guideline. Of Manchester United's three great players, Denis Law, Bobby Charlton and George Best, one was bought and two reared at Old Trafford. It's the right ratio.

So it was a particular satisfaction to find and launch Lee Sharpe and Ryan Giggs. But it was perhaps indicative of the state of our scouting system that neither player joined us through normal club channels.

I would have known nothing about Ryan until it was too late but for one of our stewards, Harold Wood. He came to me soon after I had joined the club to ask if I had heard about Ryan Wilson, then playing for Salford Schools. Ryan later took his mother's name of Giggs but he was Wilson in those days and the answer was no, we didn't know about him. I asked Brian Kidd, who was doing community work in football at that time, and he knew he was training with Manchester City. I told Joe Brown to get the lad down, and he arrived over the Christmas period.

As soon as I saw him on the pitch I knew he was a special footballer and we set out to make him a Manchester United player. We worked hard, his teachers were very good and we got the confidence of his parents. A lot of people have since laid claim to 'discovering' Ryan Giggs, but as far as Manchester United are concerned, it was all down to Harold Wood who never even claimed to be a scout!

The credit for bringing Lee Sharpe to our notice was not down to a scout either – the initial tip came from a retired journalist, Len Noad, who had moved to the Torquay area after working for most of his life in Manchester. Len told us about this youngster at the Torquay club. He had been missed in his home area of Birmingham and was a 16-year-old YTS lad in his first year. Obviously if he was any good he would get into the first-team squad and we asked Len to let us know the moment he was in the senior side.

He came on as substitute in one match and made two goals in a 2-2 draw. Tony Collins, our chief scout, watched him in his next two games and liked him. So I went down to see him against Colchester in his fifth game. I wore a bonnet and scarf and sat at the back of the stand. After about five minutes I was asked for my autograph, so obviously I would never make a spy!

We left ten minutes early and went back to the car to assess him. We agreed that though he was still very young, he had a good physique, pace and was good in the air. He had vision, awareness and it was clear after being man-marked that he was tough.

We wanted him, and knew that if we delayed there was a good chance that the Torquay manager, Cyril Knowles, would be in touch with his old club, Spurs. So we went back to the club, waited for an hour and then saw Cyril. We took him for a run in the car until he had agreed to let us have Lee.

Cyril was great and went round to see the secretary to set everything up. We stayed over at a quiet hotel on the sea front and saw Lee the next morning. He was still only 16 and we agreed to sign him on his 17th birthday. The fee was £60,000 with further payments hinged on his progress, and he played for the rest of the season at Torquay.

So there were gaps in our scouting network all right and I immediately tried to improve the situation. I wanted saturation of local football. I called meetings of clubs in the area to let them know we were there to do business, that we wanted their help in developing our scouting and in return we would do our best to help them.

As I say, Manchester City, who even had the Junior Blues – a great idea – were doing better than us. Everybody said so, even City and their Chairman Peter Swales, which was worse. Even Oldham and Crewe were doing better than us. So I called meetings of our scouts and told them I wasn't satisfied with the standard of youngster they were bringing to the club. I think they were hurt and shocked, but it had to be done. I said they must not just bring me the best boy in the street but the best in the country.

I told them I didn't want any bad players. One or two of our scouts left. I couldn't help that. One or two retired, like Eric Walker who had in fact served us well. There were a few battles which had to be fought. I brought in an extra scout in the North East and started a school of excellence in Durham after enlisting Bryan 'Pop' Robson, the former Newcastle and West Ham player to mention but two of his clubs.

So the ball was rolling. At the beginning we took gambles with players, mainly to let everyone know that Manchester United were back in business. We made sure there was decent coaching for the youngsters. People probably didn't realise what was going on but I knew it was something that had to be done. I was experienced in that area because the development of youngsters had been central to Aberdeen's success.

Archie Knox, my first signing – as assistant manager – after taking over, had been at Aberdeen with me and knew the importance of work at this level. I got Brian Kidd back to the club to help Archie set up and run a school of excellence at The Cliff training ground. It was sheer hard work but I'm sure we are reaping the benefit now with as good a set of junior players as you could hope to assemble.

At the same time in those early days I had to look at the standard of fitness at the club and I came to the conclusion that it was simply not good enough. There was no way you could expect the players to compete in 60 battles to the level demanded of Manchester United. They had to be prepared to produce in every game and I don't think they were capable of delivering. Archie, who had always worked like a beast himself, took charge of that aspect and I think it's a healthy sign that nowadays we have players responding to the necessary standard. There is a desire to win matches, coupled with flair. Winning is always important but how you win matters to the followers of Manchester United. You want the two to marry.

One of the things that shocked me when I first came down to England was a book written by Arnold Muhren, the Dutch international who had played for Ron Atkinson after signing from Ipswich. He lambasted the life-style of Manchester United players and I think he spotlighted what I felt when I assessed the dressing-room. It confirmed what Gordon Strachan had been telling me on the 'phone

25

before I had joined United. There was a lot of drinking going on behind the scenes. It was obvious there was an easy approach to their lives and a social aspect which had got out of hand. You wonder how it comes about in English football. It seems to be a part of the game here, a social sideshow which top professionals cannot really afford. I sat down and talked to the club doctor and to the staff. I wondered if it was the pressure of playing for Manchester United that created it or whether they felt that, at such a big club, it was the macho thing to do.

The one conclusion I came to without any questioning was that things had to change. All the great teams of the past used to have a drink, I'm sure, but they all went out together and it had its uses for building team spirit. I'm not puritanical but I was suspicious about the way of life at Manchester United. Socialising can do great things for the team but where it has to end is in the preparation. They have to remember who they are playing for. I stopped the lunchtime binges and made sure they knew how I felt about that aspect of their lives. There is a time to let your hair down and a time when professional footballers have to look after themselves. Players can have great careers at our club. It's great winning, it's a drug, and maybe they were not used to winning often when I first arrived.

The matter of too many older players still worried me. I wanted two centre-halves that would play for me every week, a partnership I could build the team around. I had Kevin Moran and I possibly made a mistake when I let him go the following season. He was turned 30 but was one of the best guys you could ever meet, totally committed to United. Nevertheless, he was having a lot of injuries and one of my earliest tasks was to start looking around for central defenders.

For the time being, though, I had to juggle with existing staff. We were second bottom of the League and we had to start winning a few matches to get out of the mire. Paul McGrath was injured soon after I arrived and Graeme Hogg had similar problems. At one stage I used Bryan Robson at centre-back after throwing him a challenge to which he responded very well. The centre-backs were changing all the time and though we climbed away from the foot of the table, our finishing position was a modest 11th.

I wasn't just looking around for defenders; I was trying to strengthen the whole team. One of the players I had in mind was John

Barnes and our failure to get him from Watford is still a bone of contention with me. Jesper Olsen had played quite brightly for me before going out for a couple of months with a knee injury. His contract was due to expire that summer and I wasn't sure what to do about him. So when Graham Taylor, the Watford manager, phoned me to say that Barnes was becoming available and that they were worried about him going abroad I was very interested. He phoned two or three of the top clubs like Arsenal and Liverpool. I had not seen him play myself and so I spoke to our chief scout, Tony Collins. We had only two reports on him which was a disappointment. So Tony went to watch him play against Norwich at Watford. He scored and did well. The opinion of the scouting department was that Barnes was up and down, not terribly consistent. Then he played against us at Old Trafford and did well at centre-forward. He was in my thoughts but as a relative newcomer to English football I needed guidance.

Unfortunately, I never got any strong indication from my scouts that they thought he was a player we should sign. A manager needs a chief scout who is prepared to commit himself with a firm decision for or against. Les Kershaw, who joined us later as chief scout, is prepared to throw his hat into the ring and make a judgement. I'm afraid Tony, maybe too much of the old school, was too cautious for me. Perhaps experience had made him wary, but the result for me was that we lost John Barnes to Liverpool and we have paid for it more than once. John Barnes would have been a wonderful player for Manchester United. We later parted company with Tony and I'm delighted to work with a man like Les Kershaw.

Olsen eventually left and sometimes fate works for you. Without Barnes and Olsen, Lee Sharpe and Ryan Giggs came through more quickly to the first team. They got their chances earlier, though I must say I have wondered many times about Barnes playing for Manchester United. He's a wonderful footballer and the next season he helped Liverpool to win the Championship. We only lost five games but still finished eight points behind Liverpool and Barnes was, maybe, the difference.

Kenny Dalglish made two inspired signings in Barnes and Peter Beardsley. They transformed the Liverpool team. Barnes replaced Kenny as a player and produced many magical moments. He has had a terrible year of injuries and people always seem to be talking about him being given one last chance for England. Perhaps it would be better to talk more positively and say Gary Lineker is easily England's best striker and Des Walker is the best sweeper in Europe rather than forever harping on about what Barnes has to do. He might be a worry at international level but he has been a delight for Liverpool and has probably even upstaged Ian Rush in the last couple of years. He produces great little passes. You can't rob him of the ball, you have to steal it from him rather than beat it away from him. He will simply knock you out of the road.

So we came to the end of the season and I was still looking for players. The newspapers were not short of suggestions. The People actually linked us with 104 different players in my first six months. Mind you, in my opinion that particular reporter doesn't know whether the ball is pumped or stuffed. He doesn't know anything about Manchester United. He's based in London and writes his fairy tales every weekend. I joke about it but at the time it was an extreme embarrassment for me. I used to have to phone managers to reassure them that I was not trying to negotiate behind their backs. It must also have been perhaps a disappointment to some of the players mentioned and left them wondering whether their managers were telling them the truth. You get immune to it in the end but for the first few months I was I was quite fed up with Sunday mornings.

Of course there were players who interested me. They certainly included John Barnes and I wish I had got him. I also had a go, at that time, for Gary Pallister. I saw him against Rochdale in the Milk Cup and he did very well but Tony Collins was cautious again and said we had better watch him in a higher standard of game. Sometimes, though, a manager has got to take a risk and gamble. I thought, here was someone reminiscent of Alan Hansen, quick with good feet, tall and athletic.

I phoned Bruce Rioch and asked him if he would take £400,000 for him. The Middlesbrough manager said they would be looking for at least £500,000. I might have got him for, say, £600,000 and I should have acted. Later, as we all know, I had to pay £2.3 million. That was the price of Tony's caution. He was a man who always wanted to make sure. There is no harm in that, but at the time it was not what I needed.

My priority then was to be doing something. I was also interested in Peter Beardsley and I phoned Willie McFaul, but there is something peculiar about Newcastle. You never seem to get any joy out of them, at least not Manchester United. He told me he wanted £3 million and then three weeks later they sold him to Liverpool for £1.9 million without even a phone call. I remembered then that their Chairman, Gordon McKeag, had refused to let us to speak to Paul Gascoigne. We offered the same money as Tottenham but were not allowed to approach the player. You have to think that Newcastle don't like us. Either it's just one of those things or some people are just jealous. Still, when I look at how their club is run I pity their fans. I feel sorry for our supporters not having the Championship for 25 years but their fans have even more to complain about.

I am happy to say that I had more success with one of my other transfer targets. Brian McClair was a player I knew a lot about from Scotland. Indeed, he had made a big impression on me when I was at Aberdeen. At first, when he joined Glasgow Celtic, he did not do particularly well. I recall the first time he was due to play against us and his name came up in our team talk. I said, 'Don't worry about him, he never scores against us'. He went on to score two great goals and when that sort of thing happens you sit up and take notice. I started to take particular note of his career. He was a fluid player who always moved when his team had the ball. I was impressed with his running ability and, of course, his goals. When I came down to United I knew his contract was coming up for renewal that summer and so we worked hard to get him. I have since gone in several times for players whose agreements had expired, like Mike Phelan and Neil Webb.

We also needed a full-back. John Sivebaek was a lovely lad but not really suited to the hard grind of the English season. Viv Anderson's contract was also up. So I tried to get Glenn Hysen. I had taken note of him when he had played for Gothenburg against Aberdeen. He was an impressive, strong, commanding lad and he would have done all right for us, joining at the age of about 26. I thought we had an agreement with him but he chose to go to Fiorentina and the whole situation ended as a complete farce and embarrassment for us. I don't think it did the player any good either. Later, of course, he joined Liverpool but by then I think he was over the top and not long ago he was given a free transfer. I certainly think Gary Pallister, even at his record fee, was a better investment.

I also made an enquiry about Mark Hughes who had left Manchester United to join Barcelona. Bobby Charlton and I went to watch him play for his Spanish club against Dundee United. We talked to Terry Venables but he explained that he was not in a position to let him go. He did say, though, that he would keep us in mind.

Tony Cottee was available at £2.2 million but he was not the type we needed. So I finished my first six months knowing there was a lot of work to be done and a lot of players to be signed, but I felt I had made a start to laying down foundations and letting everyone know what I was about.

Our finishing position in the League in 11th place was modest but it was better than when I arrived. We had been knocked out of the League Cup 4-1 at Southampton just prior to my appointment, a result which looked to have sealed Ron Atkinson's fate. Unhappily I couldn't claim to have made much improvement on the Cup front. We knocked out Manchester City 1-0 in the third round of the FA Cup at Old Trafford, and it is always rewarding to win a derby, but we undid all the good work by losing 1-0 at home to Coventry City in the very next round.

I went through the summer eager to get back to work and keen to see how Brian McClair would fit into our team.

THE LEGEND

SEASON 1986-87

First Division

	P	W	D	L	F	A	PTS
Everton	42	26	8	8	76	31	86
Liverpool	42	23	8	11	72	42	77
Tottenham Hotspur	42	21	8	13	68	43	71
Arsenal	42	20	10	12	58	35	70
Norwich City	42	17	17	8	53	51	68
Wimbledon	42	19	9	14	57	50	66
Luton Town	42	18	12	12	47	45	66
Nottingham Forest	42	18	11	13	64	51	65
Watford	42	18	9	15	67	54	63
Coventry City	42	17	12	13	50	45	63
MANCHESTER UNITED	42	14	14	14	52	45	56
Southampton	42	14	10	18	69	68	52
Sheffield Wednesday	42	13	13	16	58	59	52
Chelsea	42	13	13	16	53	64	52
West Ham United	42	14	10	18	52	67	52
Queens Park Rangers	42	13	11	18	48	64	50
Newcastle United	42	12	11	19	47	65	47
Oxford United	42	11	13	18	44	69	46
Charlton Athletic	42	11	11	20	45	55	44
Leicester City	42	11	9	22	54	76	42
Manchester City	42	8	15	19	36	57	39
Aston Villa	42	8	12	22	45	79	36

APPEARANCES

	League	Littlewoods Cup	FA Cup	Total
Peter Davenport	34(5)	4	1(1)	39(6)
Paul McGrath	34(1)	4	0(1)	38(1)
Gordon Strachan	33(1)	2	2	37(1)
Mike Duxbury	32	3	2	37
Kevin Moran	32(1)	2(1)	2	36(2)
Norman Whiteside	31	3(1)	2	36(1)
Bryan Robson	29(1)	3	0	32(1)
Frank Stapleton	25(9)	4	2	31(9)
John Sivebaek	27(1)	1	2	30(1)
Chris Turner	23	4	2	29
Colin Gibson	24	1	1	26
Jesper Olsen	22(6)	1(1)	2	25(7)
Arthur Albiston	19(3)	4	0	23(3)
Remi Moses	17(1)	4	0	21(1)
Gary Walsh	14	0	0	14
Terry Gibson	12(4)	0(2)	1(1)	13(7)
Graeme Hogg	11	2	0	13
Clayton Blackmore	10(2)	0	2	11(2)
Billy Garton	9	0	2	11
Liam O'Brien	9(2)	0	0	9(2)
Peter Barnes	7	2	0	9
Gary Bailey	5	0	0	5
Nicky Wood	2	0(1)	0	2(1)
Tony Gill	1	0	0	1

GOALSCORERS

	League	Littlewoods Cup	FA Cup	Total
Peter Davenport	14(inc 4 pens)	2(inc 1 pen)	0	16(inc 5 pens)
Norman Whiteside	8	1	1	10
Frank Stapleton	7	2	0	9
Bryan Robson	7	0	0	7
Gordon Strachan	4	0	0	4
Jesper Olsen	3(inc 1 pen)	0	0	3(inc 1 pen)
Paul McGrath	2	0	0	2
Remi Moses	0	2	0	2
Peter Barnes	0	1	0	1
Clayton Blackmore	1	0	0	1
Mike Duxbury	1	0	0	1
Colin Gibson	1	0	0	1
Terry Gibson	1	0	0	1
John Sivebaek	1	0	0	1
Own Goals	2	0	0	2
Total	52 (inc 5 pens)	8 (inc 1 pen)	1	61(inc 6 pens)

FA CUP

Round 3	Manchester City	(H)	W	1-0
Round 4	Coventry City	(H)	L	0-1

LEAGUE CUP

Round 2/1	Port Vale	(H)	W	2-0
Round 2/2	Port Vale	(A)	W	5-2
Round 3	Southampton	(H)	D	0-0
Round 3 Replay	Southampton	(A)	L	1-4

Chapter Three

COLLISION COURSE

If Norman Whiteside had had one more yard of pace he would have been one of the greatest players ever produced in British football; but for continuous knee problems affecting him, he would without doubt have become a truly world-class star. As it was he still managed to make a tremendous impact on English football and was outstanding for both Manchester United and Northern Ireland in his early days. He had incredible quality, an ice-cold temperament and he could play easily on any stage. If you looked at his eyes, he just stared through opponents as if they were not there. He had wonderful vision and a good touch on the ball, all topped off with that infamous aggressive streak which often had supporters as well as opponents cringing.

To reflect on the whole saga of Norman's troubles and his departure from Manchester United would almost fill a book on its own. Suffice to say, we had an enormous problem relating to his off-field behaviour, a situation compounded by Paul McGrath causing similar worries around the same time and which had both men on collision courses with me.

My first concern was that I had to get rid of this idea that Manchester United were a drinking club, rather than a football club. I knew that if we were to have United meeting the vision and expectations of supporters, as a club of class and style, somewhere in the profile there had to be discipline. Without that discipline, all the other talents can go fluttering off in a million directions.

I would have to separate Norman and Paul, though it would always be as a pair that they seemed to hit the newspaper headlines, and it was as a pair that they eventually left Old Trafford. In the case of Norman, I have nothing but the greatest admiration for him and I sincerely believe that most of his problem was down to disappointment and possibly depression with his continual injury. I believe he sought refuge in a lifestyle which, of course, created conflict with my concept of a Manchester United player.

It is fair to say that I would have preferred to have kept him but an example had to be made to the rest of the club. Norman was younger than Paul, which posed the question of whether I should persevere with him. He tried to force the issue at one stage by asking for a transfer. For a short spell it alienated him from supporters which I'm sure came as a big shock to him. Eventually, the situation reached a climax and I think at the end of the day Norman would be the first to agree that the action I took was right for the club and right for him. I am sure he would acknowledge now that it is not Alex Ferguson who is important but how I believe the club should be run. United are more important than any of us and it was with that in mind that I knew I had to act to make everyone aware of what was expected of a Manchester United player.

I was always sympathetic to him and I did my best to talk him into a better standard for himself and for the club. That sympathy still exists, reflected in the decision to grant him a testimonial match against Everton at the end of last season.

However, although having a sympathy of a kind for Paul McGrath, it was a quite different relationship. I sensed that he was on a self-destruct course. I don't know when it started but it was gathering momentum by the time I reached Old Trafford.

Whether he lacked intelligence to understand what was happening or whether he had gone too far down the road to ruin, I'm not sure. The sad part for me, among many sadnesses with the whole situation, was that I didn't register with him. Popular opinion seems to have it that after he had moved to Aston Villa, Graham Taylor found the right way to handle him, giving him a professional minder, more medical help and the like.

I must tell you, we offered him every facility and advice we could think of. Sir Matt Busby spoke to him along with the club doctor,

Francis McHugh, and we even got his parish priest in to try and help. We tried every avenue to make Paul understand he was ruining his career. I even spoke to his wife several times. My conclusion from all this was that I was battering my head against a brick wall.

In separating the two of them I would also have to say that Norman was far more intelligent and understood everything you said to him. Paul I was never sure about because you never got any dialogue with him. He just nodded his head, agreed with everything you said, left the room and continued on his merry way. Nothing I said or did seemed to matter to him.

If there was a climax in Paul's United career resulting in him also asking for a transfer, it was the car crash after one of his spectacular nights out. After his discharge from hospital I couldn't actually muster any anger with him. I was just happy he was alive and there was no need at that point to go into any rage because he had suffered enough.

I suppose even in the darkest days there was a funny side. I will never forget the week in which Paul and Norman made a tour of Manchester's clubs and pubs. It was a journey charted by supporters phoning in to let me know where they were and the state they were in on their merry-go-round. It was like a treasure trail. The important difference between them was that Paul was supposed to be in the team at the end of that week against Queens Park Rangers whereas Norman was out with injury. Come the Friday before the game, after I don't know how many reprimands, Paul couldn't train. On the Saturday, he refused to play against QPR, saying he wasn't fit enough, which I suppose was inevitable under the circumstances.

It meant, though, that I had to call in Deiniol Graham as my thirteenth man after he had played in the 'A' team at Preston on Saturday morning – not a very professional situation. It had been quite a week and it finally drained all my patience. It was a situation which had eaten at my trust and confidence in professional footballers. So many people in the game refer to the need for a manager to hold the respect of his players. I consider it just as important for the players to have the respect of their manager. Therein lay the foundation for my decision to let Paul go.

Everyone around the club knew I didn't approve of the way of life of either player and that they didn't see eye to eye with my decisions.

They weren't the kind of players I was used to having about me. Possibly if I had been older I would have been more tolerant. Actually I hope I wouldn't be, but you never know, I may turn out that way. The main thing is that I didn't want people to get the impression that drinking was part of life with Manchester United. It had to be accepted that we are a football club and that everyone was there to do justice to themselves out on the pitch.

I also believed very firmly that when a lot of people have spent a lot of money they are entitled to see the players demonstrating that they have the same kind of caring for Manchester United. I felt I had to let everyone know that that was what the standard was about at Old Trafford. In short, I wasn't prepared to tolerate a way of life which in my book fell short.

Don't get me wrong. There is nothing wrong with having a drink. After all I once ran a pub, but for professional footballers it has to be in moderation, at least on the run-up to matches when they must be properly prepared. I like to think that both Norman and Paul would agree now that I was right and that a stand had to be made.

One aspect that particularly disappointed me was that Paul chose to lambast me in a Sunday newspaper. Norman, when he left, did not say a word and he has my respect for that. In turn, I don't want to go into all the gory details of the rows we had, the phone calls I had about their activities and the trouble I had tracking them down at times.

Once the wheels were set in motion for them to go Graham Taylor phoned from Aston Villa to ask me about Paul. He wanted to know if I thought he was worth taking. I gave him a definite yes and explained that I was letting him go simply because of the way things had developed and that I had to change the image of the club. Then when Colin Harvey called about Norman I said the same thing – that he had to go because our relationship had been spoiled and that a break was needed. I also told him that the pair of them needed splitting up.

Norman's knee had cleared up and I believed that a fresh challenge would work wonders for him. He did indeed start off brilliantly at Goodison Park, scoring 14 or 15 goals in his first season, including one against Manchester United! I had wished him all the best when he left and was pleased with his success at Everton.

With Paul it was slightly more acrimonious. I would have wished him well, too, but I never got the opportunity. The details of his transfer to Villa Park were negotiated on the phone from Bryan Robson's house during a Sunday barbecue and he never came near Old Trafford again. I wish he had done because then I could have explained why I had taken the action I did and made him understand it was best for both him and Manchester United.

It was really for his own good, but that did not stop him attacking me in the paper the next week, and he was totally out of order. *The News of the World* makes a practice of trying to get players leaving United to write a knocking piece. They also did it with Graeme Hogg and Peter Barnes. It was laughable with Peter because when I arrived he wrote a piece saying it was time Ron Atkinson left, which incidentally I had him on the mat about. But when Peter left the club he did another article saying that the worst thing that had happened to Manchester United was Ron Atkinson leaving.

Peter was always a bit mixed up, though. He blames the game for changing because he didn't fancy the idea of working back as a winger. He totally failed to realise that all the great players have worked. Ruud Gullitt works as hard as the rest of his team and I recall that they once put a pedometer on Di Stefano and found that he covered more ground than anyone else in the Real Madrid team. Players like Cruyff, George Best and Bobby Charlton went from penalty box to penalty box and I have often wondered why Peter Barnes felt he was different.

I have rather run ahead of myself, though, to complete the story of Norman Whiteside and Paul McGrath. My first reaction when Paul started to miss games was to look at the centre-back position. He started season 1987-88 off very well but began to have trouble with his knee in mid-October and he missed 18 matches. We had very little in the way of back-up. Billy Garton had had an injury or two so he was struggling, while Graeme Hogg was continually out with a pelvic problem. Paul's knee injury had started soon after I had arrived the previous season when he had been caught in a late tackle by Clive Allen in a televised 3-3 game against Spurs.

I just didn't have consistency of appearances among the centre-backs with Kevin Moran also playing in only half the games that season. So in the December I went for Steve Bruce. I had had my eye on him for some time. I saw him play for Norwich against Watford and Manchester City. I always thought of him as a player born out of sheer enthusiasm which he also generated in his team. For his height he attacked the ball well in the air and he had fair pace. I considered him a more than capable deputy for McGrath. Most importantly, though, I needed somebody to play every week and I have certainly not been disappointed on that score.

Injuries were part and parcel of my first couple of years. Take, for instance, Viv Anderson. I had signed him from Arsenal during the summer along with McClair from Celtic. I think he had missed two games in four years at Highbury and that was through suspension. I spoke to Don Howe and couldn't have got a better testimony. Bobby Robson was equally full of praise. I knew he was out of contract that summer and therefore available. At £250,000, a fee fixed by the League tribunal, he was a marvellous bit of business. George Graham was certainly not pleased with the fee, even though he only bought him from Nottingham Forest for £200,000.

When you buy a player you always try to examine his attitude to life and Viv had a marvellous pedigree. He still always shoves that big smiling face round the dressing-room door when he visits Old Trafford, which he often does. Even after he joined Sheffield Wednesday I wanted to take him on a European trip because it's great to have him around. Unfortunately, he had a commitment at Hillsborough which prevented him from joining us. He is very much a role model for young professionals. Unhappily, you can't be lucky all the time with injuries and soon after joining us he started to pick up a knock or two. Then the following season he was struck down with mysterious heel and hip difficulties. He hardly played at all. Ironically, since moving to Sheffield Wednesday he has hardly been injured again.

My first full season at Old Trafford was the time for me to examine my attitude to the club. There were so many roads to go down and so many things I wanted to do. The place was unbelievable and what I tried to do was make people aware of what I was about.

As manager I didn't want people to think I was divorced from them and living in an aloof ivory tower. I also didn't want to change.

I didn't want to gather hangers-on about me or encircle myself with new-found friends who are always about football clubs. I had heard about the reputation of United as a showbiz club and sometimes on a Saturday you can get the impression of a ritzy set-up. I believe it's largely false because behind the glitter there is a tremendous affection for the club from the people who follow it and especially from those who work for it. It infects you. It's one of those clubs run, to a degree, by the supporters because it is high-profile and there are a lot of them not slow to make their feelings known. The club must listen to them.

Martin Edwards, the Chairman, gets criticised but I must say that after all my years with Aberdeen, Manchester United always attach significance to what the supporters are thinking. Ken Ramsden, the assistant secretary, seems to keep a special ear to the ground and at staff meetings he regularly brings up what supporters are saying and thinking, be it concern over Cup tickets, price rises or any of the other matters which worry the fans. Perhaps he has this sensitive touch because he has worked for the club since he was a boy and even his mother worked here. He can reflect the supporters' views. It's something I try to understand myself, as well, and I can honestly say that, in the main, there is always good intention from the board in relation to supporters.

In those early days I also had to come to terms with the media. It would be true to say that it has been one of my hassles and that until I won the FA Cup there seemed to be incessant speculation about players I was supposed to be signing.

I had a lot of sorting out to do that season, and I don't just mean Paul McGrath and Norman Whiteside. I wondered about little Terry Gibson when I first arrived. He was out of the side and I brought him back against Arsenal in the January. He scored a goal to help us give the Gunners their first defeat of the season. I gave him a run of seven or eight games but he didn't score again and he never quite managed to convince either himself or me that he was at the right club. Very often, if players don't settle at Old Trafford, they just melt. It takes presence to handle the stage and Terry was one of those who never quite adjusted. He had a lovely change of pace, a powerful shot in both feet and he was more than a reasonable player. But he was never going to beat the barrier. I think he admitted it himself after he left. The nice thing is that he won an FA Cup medal with Wimbledon after leaving us. I always like players to do well when they leave me, though I wasn't too happy when he helped Wimbledon knock us out of the League Cup two years later by scoring twice in an infamous match at Plough Lane.

I think my assessment of Terry, while harsh perhaps, was still fair. As a manager you must separate the essentials from trivia and pick teams to win matches rather than simply players whom you like. There has always got to be a mix of personalities in a dressing-room. Apart from the fact that it is probably inevitable anyway, it is the right thing to have. There has to be the studious one, the flamboyant type, the thinker, the battler. At the end of the day it is the personality and presence they show on the field that matters, and it can often be quite different from their character off it.

For instance you couldn't get a word out of Remi Moses until he went out on the pitch, when he would immediately start yapping and continue to rabbit away all through the game. Ryan Giggs is another who changes dramatically once the whistle goes. He is so shy off the field but his personality changes during a game of football when he uses the pitch to project his innermost self and he becomes a steely-eyed winner, full of confidence and bold in his football.

Watching a boy like Giggs coming through is one of the joys of being a manager, and conversely telling a young man that he isn't going to make it is undoubtedly the hardest part of the job. For that matter it isn't easy letting any player go. My consoling thought is that I hope I have done something for the boys who leave, that they have benefited in some way from being a part of Manchester United. There is always the odd exception but you hope they will do well at their next club or in life if it is the end of their playing careers. You certainly don't want them to fail simply because you are moving them on. I keep in touch with a lot of my old players and always get a Christmas card from the likes of Chris Turner, Kevin Moran and Peter Davenport, lovely people, good professionals, good Manchester United players ... and on they go to fresh challenges.

The attitude of a few of the others puzzles and hurts you, like the ones who blast away in newspaper articles and you wonder whether they have fanned the flames of their resentment simply to spice up their articles and make more money. Colin Gibson, for instance, wrote a piece and said I very nearly drove him to drink. I couldn't believe it when I recalled how much time I had spent on him. He was a terrible worrier and day after day, week after week, I tried to talk him through his doubts and problems. I couldn't have done more for the boy. He certainly hasn't had the best of luck in his career with more injuries since leaving us, I see.

But for every one you seem to fail to help, there are countless more you have been able to help. I was delighted later, for instance, that I was able to recommend Tony Gill to Martin Dobson following the boy's early retirement from football with a badly broken leg, and he became the youth coach at Bristol Rovers to get a start on the staff side of the game.

Another satisfying moment around this time was being able to give Gary Walsh his debut. The staff had told me about Gary's great performance in the FA Youth Cup final against Manchester City and he had been getting glowing reports in the reserves. I brought him in six weeks after my arrival, at Villa Park. We went into a 3-1 lead and ended with a 3-3 draw. It was a really exciting game and the first involving Manchester United to give me a real big game feeling. The atmosphere was electric and it was a good test for Gary in more ways than one. Apart from the tension, he faced a fierce baptism of fire from Andy Gray and Garry Thompson, a bomber crew if ever there was one. Very early on he made a great save low down with his left hand from Thompson and he went on to take all the challenges hurled at him. I said to myself at the time: 'He'll do for me!'

Since then, of course, he has suffered ill luck with injuries. He came back to finish the season as the goalkeeper in possession of the jersey and he started off the next season for a run of 16 games. He took a bad bang on the head in a dramatic game at Sheffield Wednesday which we won 4-2. He did well to carry on, as did Kevin Moran who also had concussion. Gary played a few more matches until we had a gap in the fixtures and I took the team for a break in Barbados, not the happiest of decisions as it turned out.

It certainly wasn't for Gary, who got a second head injury as the result of a terribly crude challenge by the centre-forward of the local team. It put him out for the rest of the season, but it wasn't the end of his bad luck. The following pre-season we let him go to Gordon McQueen at Airdrie to get his touch back and he came back with an ankle injury. Then followed a whole series of attempted come-backs before a surgeon marvellously saved his career with a pioneering operation involving a bone graft.

The dependable Chris Turner finished the season and then because we didn't know when Gary would be back I signed Jim Leighton. More recently, of course, I signed Peter Schmeichel, which undoubtedly disappointed Gary and as events have proved, it has reduced his chances of first-team football at Old Trafford.

I had a long chat with Gary at the time of the Schmeichel signing, though, and explained that I needed an experienced goalkeeper straight away because the club had waited long enough for the Championship and we were going to make a major attempt to capture it. I know Gary will have a big career in the game. His time will come and I have promised him that if a big club comes in for him we won't stand in his way. If I feel we have adequate cover for him at the time I will let him go, reluctantly I might add, because he is an outstanding young goalkeeper, but in fairness to a boy who through no fault of his own has seen his career at Old Trafford marking time. I have given him that promise and I'll keep it. I know that if I were to transfer him tomorrow to a reasonable First Division club he would get an England cap inside two years. In the meantime I hope he is enjoying life at United. He should because he is with the biggest club in the game.

Not every player is able to come back from serious injury and one of Gary's equally promising team-mates in the junior sides had to quit. Nicky Wood was a great prospect, which I quickly recognised, and I played him in the April of my first season against Nottingham Forest and Oxford. He had good pace and he was a clever winger with a trick or two for beating full-backs. We won both games and he was excellent. I waited for him throughout the following season but he never played again. It subsequently turned out that he had an endemic back problem but it baffled our medical people for a long time. He seemed to have no stamina and when he complained he was struggling we even wondered whether he was making excuses. It all stemmed from his back trouble and eventually he had to give up playing at professional level, very sad. At least we learned something and we do more detailed medical checks now designed to diagnose this kind of complaint.

My first full season saw me having to make a number of difficult decisions at both junior and senior levels. Arthur Albiston had grown up at the club and was United through and through, but he was another topping 30 years old and, as I explained earlier, we simply had too many of them at the club. I had to get the average age down. He had played in my first game at Oxford and then had to drop out with injury and he didn't get back until near the end of the season.

That summer he had an operation for a hernia, the source of long-standing trouble, but Mike Duxbury and Viv Anderson were the full-backs and on Arthur's occasional appearances I don't think he played to the level he wanted. He never really seemed to recapture his form for us after the operation. At the end of the season I let him go. He was a tremendous wee pro though and always liked to play. I was happy that both he and Kevin Moran had testimonials as well as being able to continue their careers elsewhere.

Arthur subsequently played for West Bromwich, Dundee and Chester while Kevin went to Spain and then Blackburn. I am sure their friends think I let them leave too early, but I firmly believe that if you cannot honestly see real first-team prospects any longer for players of their experience it is fairer to release them. If I had kept those particular players back for another year they might well have lost their edge playing in our reserves and then not made such good moves. Kevin even continued to play for the Republic of Ireland. I believe you owe your long-serving players that kind of consideration.

With Brain McClair settling quickly into his scoring stride and Norman Whiteside knocking in a couple on the opening day at Southampton, we made quite a good start to the 1987-88 season. In fact at the end of August we were top of the League, but I still told the Chairman that I didn't feel we were good enough to win the Championship.

September rather bore me out with a couple of draws and a defeat to leave victory at home to Spurs our only full-pointer. We only lost five League games all season, but we didn't enjoy Cup runs of note, going out of both the FA Cup and Rumbelows Cup in the fifth rounds.

Liverpool, on the other hand, were their usual consistent selves. We drew 1-1 with them at Old Trafford and 3-3 at Anfield, so honours were even in that respect, but overall you could not class us as good as Liverpool. They stumbled a bit towards the end and we caught fire to win eight of our last ten games, drawing the other two. We had some good results and some exciting ones. We scored four in four games, with McClair featuring strongly on the scoresheet. He notched twice in both fixtures against Sheffield Wednesday, then against Portsmouth and grabbed his first hat-trick for the club at home to Derby County.

So it was an encouraging close to my first full season but the difference between ourselves and Liverpool was reflected in the First Division table. Liverpool were champions with 89 points. Yes, we were runners-up, but eight points behind. I didn't like it and I wondered whether it was time to break up the team and buy.

On the money side, I didn't have unlimited resources. The Chairman and board at Old Trafford have always backed their managers financially, but you have to act responsibly as well. You certainly do if you are aiming, like me, to stay with the club for many years. It means you spend for the future and plan prudently. So I knew that I would have to bring in some cash if I was going to embark on any big buys, and I knew it would take a few bob if I was to realise my ambition of bringing Mark Hughes back to the club.

I started to prune, with the result that we said goodbye to Chris Turner, Arthur Albiston, Kevin Moran, Graeme Hogg and John Sivebaek. In addition Gary Bailey and Remi Moses quit because of injury and we got insurance payouts for the players personally as well as for the club. I was also looking for a buyer for Jesper Olsen and he went early the next season. I must say I would never offload so extensively again, because as I was to discover the hard way, I had cut us to the bone and ambitious clubs need big squads if they are to challenge on more than one front.

But at least it brought some cash in to finance the buying of a new goalkeeper and a striker. I got Jim Leighton, who had served me brilliantly at Aberdeen, for £450,000 and brought my summer spending to the £2 million mark by bringing Mark Hughes home from exile in Spain.

As I mentioned before, I had tried for Mark the previous year and had been refused by Terry Venables. Now the situation seemed different. Barcelona had had him out on loan with Bayern Munich, so obviously there had been a problem at Nou Camp. My own feeling is that he should never have been allowed to leave in the first place, but it is obviously unfair of me to criticise because I wasn't the manager at the time and I don't know all the facts.

Certainly Mark's contract was coming to an end at Old Trafford when he joined Barcelona, but I do wonder what part the agent played in his transfer. The modern agent is a relatively new animal who has to be handled very carefully and in some cases with great caution and even suspicion. What I do think was that the deal should not have been conducted during the season. If the boy chose to try his luck abroad, fine, but nothing should have been finalised until the close season. It's not fair to the supporters.

I have been involved in a few controversial decisions involving popular players and only in time does the support begin to understand a manager and his judgements. Anyway, my big concern was to get him back and the price quoted us by the agent was very attractive. It was an upward trend for strikers and Peter Beardsley was being quoted at £3 million.

So, even taking into account the difficult time he had had abroad, the asking price for Mark at £1 million seemed a snip. I might add that towards the end of the negotiations, the fee suddenly jumped to £1.4 million, which right at the death mysteriously became £1.6 million, and I wonder just what the agent had to do with that creeping transfer price. But you cannot let the fans down after all the expectation and so we smiled and paid up.

We certainly approached the next season in optimistic mood.

SEASON 1987-88

	P	W	D	L	F	A	PTS
Liverpool	40	26	12	2	87	24	90
MANCHESTER UNITED	40	23	12	5	71	38	81
Nottingham Forest	40	20	13	7	67	39	73
Everton	40	19	13	8	53	27	70
Queens Park Rangers	40	19	10	11	48	38	67
Arsenal	40	18	12	10	58	39	66
Wimbledon	40	14	15	11	58	47	57
Newcastle United	40	14	14	12	55	53	56
Luton Town	40	14	11	15	57	58	53
Coventry City	40	13	14	13	46	53	53
Sheffield Wednesday	40	15	8	17	52	66	53
Southampton	40	12	14	14	49	53	50
Tottenham Hotspur	40	12	11	17	38	48	47
Norwich City	40	12	9	19	40	52	45
Derby County	40	10	13	17	35	45	43
West Ham United	40	9	15	16	40	52	42
Charlton Athletic	40	9	15	16	38	52	42
Chelsea	40	9	15	16	50	68	42
Portsmouth	40	7	14	19	36	66	35
Watford	40	7	11	22	27	51	32
Oxford United	40	6	13	21	44	80	31

APPEARANCES

	League	Littlewoods Cup	FA Cup	Total
Brian McClair	40	5	3	48
Mike Duxbury	39	5	3	47
Bryan Robson	36	5	2	43
Gordon Strachan	33(3)	5	3	41(3)
Viv Anderson	30(1)	4	3	37(1)
Jesper Olsen	30(7)	3(1)	2(1)	35(9)
Norman Whiteside	26(1)	5	3	34(1)
Colin Gibson	26(3)	5	2	33(3)
Chris Turner	24	3	3	30
Peter Davenport	21(13)	3(1)	1(1)	25(15)
Steve Bruce	21	0	3	24
Paul McGrath	21(1)	2	0	23(1)
Kevin Moran	20(1)	2	1	23(1)
Clayton Blackmore	15(7)	3(1)	1(1)	19(9)
Remi Moses	16(1)	1(1)	1	18(2)
Gary Walsh	16	2	0	18
Graeme Hogg	9(1)	0(1)	2	11(2)
Billy Garton	5(1)	2(1)	0	7(2)
Liam O'Brien	6(11)	0(2)	0(2)	6(15)
Arthur Albiston	5(6)	0	0	5(6)
Deiniol Graham	1	0(1)	0	1(1)
Lee Martin	0(1)	0	0	0(1)

GOALSCORERS

	League	Littlewoods Cup	FA Cup	Total
Brian McClair	24 (inc 5 pens)	5 (inc 1 pen)	2	31 (inc 6 pens)
Bryan Robson	11	0	0	11
Norman Whiteside	7	2	1	10
Gordon Strachan	8	1	0	9
Peter Davenport	5	1	0	6
Viv Anderson	2	0	1	3
Clayton Blackmore	3	0	0	3
Paul McGrath	2	1	0	3
Steve Bruce	2	0	0	2
Colin Gibson	2	0	0	2
Liam O'Brien	2	0	0	2
Jesper Olsen	2	0	0	2
Own Goals	1	0	1	2
Total	71 (inc 5 pens)	10 (inc 1 pen)	5	86 (inc 6 pens)

FA CUP

Round 3	Ipswich	(A)	W	2-1
Round 4	Chelsea	(H)	W	2-0
Round 5	Arsenal	(A)	L	1-2

LEAGUE CUP

Round 2/1	Hull City	(H)	W	5-0
Round 2/2	Hull City	(A)	W	1-0
Round 3	Crystal Palace	(H)	W	2-1
Round 4	Bury	(A)*	W	2-1
Round 5	Oxford	(A)	L	0-2

* Played at Old Trafford

Chapter Four

MOMENT OF DECISION

Should I have let Gordon Strachan leave Manchester United?

I am sure there are plenty of people who would argue that Strachan's transfer to Leeds United was in fact the biggest mistake of my career. Certainly wee Gordon had the last laugh when Leeds pipped us for the Championship after he became a key figure in the Elland Road set-up. But with hand on heart I can honestly say that allowing Gordon to move on was the right thing to do, and that subsequent events have not altered the opinion I held at the time.

There would have been no point keeping Gordon Strachan. Basically, he had run out of steam for Manchester United and to have kept him would have been a waste of time for both us and him.

I think I know him better than anyone in football because, of course, he played for me at Aberdeen and it seemed a small world when I was appointed Manager at Old Trafford to find I was his boss again. I don't really know how Gordon felt because we had a few stormy encounters at Pittodrie. Most of them have been exaggerated since and become part of soccer's folklore, but it's true the teacups did once fly in his direction at half-time in a game at Aberdeen!

The beginning of the end for Gordon at Old Trafford came in season 1988-89. In my view he had not been performing for us to the standard expected of any Manchester United player, and compared to the player I knew of old he was only a shadow of his former self. I knew what made him tick. He needed to be motivated and I eventually ran out of ideas to keep him playing to the full range of his ability. I certainly tried hard enough. I was always looking for opportunities in my pre-match talks to elevate him and make him feel vital.

Matters came to a head when we were knocked out of the FA Cup at home to Nottingham Forest in the sixth round. I had gone out of my way to build him up for that Cup-tie. He had given me the opportunity a few weeks previously by playing particularly well in a 3-1 win against West Ham when he had scored his first League goal of the season. I kept hammering home the message that the wee man was back on form and was the guy to take us to Wembley.

Gordon has since said that he felt I had lost faith in him. It's a nonsense because I praised him plenty. All the management did. I don't consider I failed in my duty to Gordon Strachan in terms of motivating him to play. It's often been said since his move to Leeds that he inspired the club. Perhaps he did, but with the money we were paying him I think we were entitled to expect him to inspire us with the enormous ability he had.

When we were at Aberdeen he was always saying he was bored and perhaps he slipped into a similar state with Manchester United after his proposed move to France had fallen through. He has also since said that he knew we had been interested in Trevor Steven and he was right. It may have affected him, thinking he would have competition from a younger man. No-one is likely to know because Gordon would never tell you exactly what he was thinking.

The question of players expecting to be motivated all the time worries me because quite frankly, in my view, it is too easy for them to turn round and blame the manager when they have not performed. It can be a cop-out! I wonder what miners and shipyard workers think. Are they always saying: 'Please, Boss, hurry up and motivate me before I go down the pit or keel a boat in the freezing cold?'

I think they would feel that £100,000 a year is plenty of motivation.

But whatever the reasons for Gordon losing heart with us, I don't think I need to defend myself. We did our best for him, but like Frank Stapleton before him, perhaps he was simply coming to the end of his days with us. Leeds took him but perhaps we need better players than Leeds because of the expectations at Old Trafford.

Don't get me wrong about Gordon. He is a likeable lad and we miss his bubbly personality in the dressing-room, but I feel he used his book to put the blame on me for his departure when by rights he should have been examining his own performances and contribution when he was a Manchester United player.

I take nothing away from what he has achieved at Leeds. He is a credit to himself with the way he has looked after his fitness and he is a fine example to all young professionals, but I have never regretted him going because he had no more to offer Manchester United. I know him and he needed to leave. He has said as much himself and in his video he actually admits he took it easy with us for a year, but I wonder if he ever considers that he let himself down when he was at Old Trafford. In my opinion he should have done better than he did, and blaming me is not the answer for him. It had nothing to do with Alex Ferguson and it saddens me when players look to blame the manager for not motivating them.

You have only to study Bryan Robson to discover the right attitude. Isn't he a joy to behold, how he bursts himself to win games? Has there ever been a game he has not tried his utmost to win or given everything? That's the true example of a great player, still hungry at the age of 35 and ready for more.

Gordon was a big star at Aberdeen and he is that again at Leeds. At Old Trafford he was just one one of a lot of major players and perhaps that was his problem.

As I admit, we had our rows, more probably at Aberdeen than at Old Trafford, but if I lose my temper it is for a reason. For one thing I care very deeply about things. I remember Jock Stein saying 'Always wait until Monday so you can give a studied response to a match,' but I couldn't do that to save my life. I have to get things out of my system. It's in my make-up. I'm perhaps a little more patient now, more understanding, if you like. I have improved, but there are some aspects I hope I will never change.

I never give in or give up easily on either a player or a cause. Even if the team have won I'm not always happy because standards are all-important to me and if they have dropped I'm angry. Very few players seem able to find that level of self-motivation and discipline, but Manchester United are getting there and we have a few real winners at the club now. I keep drumming it into them so that hopefully they will become part of me, mirroring my own determination.

I decided to sell Gordon on the Monday after our defeat in the sixth round of the FA Cup against Nottingham Forest at Old Trafford. He had almost gone to a French club the previous summer but had changed his mind at the last minute. I am not hanging our 0-1 defeat entirely round Gordon's neck, but he was 32 and hadn't done much all season. He had also been telling people in the dressing-room that he intended leaving at the end of the season.

Ron Atkinson phoned at 9.30 on the Monday morning. He really gave me time to get over the Cup blow! He asked about Gordon but I said he was not available because I had promised Howard Wilkinson at Leeds first refusal on him.

I rang Howard and told him the situation and he said he was interested but had just taken a phone call from Ron who had told him not to bother because Sheffield Wednesday were buying him. I explained that that wasn't exactly the position and that he had first option because of our agreement. I asked for £300,000 because Gordon's contract was up at the end of the season when of course he would fetch a lot less than that figure at his age.

I contacted Gordon and told him Leeds were in for him. He said bluntly he didn't fancy a Second Division club and that from what he had heard about Leeds he didn't want to go there. I told him it would do him no harm to speak to Howard and that they might offer him the moon. So he phoned Howard, who very cleverly got him over to Elland Road. It was an ace move because as I was driving past their ground on my way to Middlesbrough to watch Gary Pallister, my car phone went.

It was Gordon on the line to say that not only had Leeds offered him the moon, it was two moons, plus the sun and Mars. So he signed for Leeds and I still believe a move was right for both us and him. He needed a jolt, just like Paul McGrath, and it triggered him back to life and the kind of form he had not shown in Manchester for a long time.

The start to that season had not been bad. We drew at home on the opening day to QPR with a team which lined up: Leighton, Blackmore, Martin, Bruce, McGrath, McClair, Robson, Strachan, Davenport, Hughes, Olsen. Sub: O'Brien. We played an experimental five at the back, with Bryan Robson sweeping. Then Liverpool beat us 1-0 with a John Barnes penalty. But we picked up to win the next three games. It was high tempo stuff and I concluded we were not bad. We had strength up front with Brian McClair and Mark Hughes while at the back Steve Bruce was settling nicely alongside Paul McGrath.

But then Paul McGrath had one of his injuries which kept him out for about 17 games. Kevin Moran had been transferred because we had Billy Garton coming along and he replaced Paul. Unhappily he fell ill with what eventually proved to be the mysterious ME disease, which leaves sufferers weak and prone to all kinds of debilitating symptoms. It's certainly a problem for a professional footballer and perhaps in the early days no-one really understood fully Billy's difficulties which eventually forced his retirement.

The immediate problem for me was that I had been left with just one natural centre-back which is why I went out and bought Mal Donaghy from Luton. He made his debut for us in a 1-1 draw at Everton when Mark Hughes scored one of his famous volleys. Mal has been a tremendous player for us, coming in and out of the team with never a complaint. He played in every match for the rest of that season and got us out of a big hole.

We carried on for the rest of the season, not doing too badly, nothing brilliant mind you, but we had too many draws to make any challenge in the League. Bryan Robson played in most of the games, but we didn't get many appearances from Viv Anderson, Billy Garton, Colin Gibson, Norman Whiteside, Paul McGrath or Mike Duxbury. In fact we had only three players who played the whole season with a couple more quite close.

I said to the directors quite early on that it wouldn't be our year for the Championship. We were too erratic and in selling players to raise money towards buying Sparky Hughes I had left us thin on the ground when injuries struck. But at least it did give me the opportunity to introduce a batch of our young ones and the season will always remain in my mind for our FA Cup run and the part 'Fergie's Fledglings' played in it.

Lads like Lee Martin, Tony Gill, Russell Beardsmore, Mark Robins, David Wilson and Deiniol Graham all appeared and fired the imagination of the supporters. I was excited myself and we had three great tussles with QPR in the third round. We could only manage a goalless draw in the first game and not many people fancied us for the replay in

London. The kids had a field day though, taking us to 2-2 in extra time with Gill and Graham the scorers. We won the second replay comfortably enough, 3-0, with the older players, Brian McClair and Bryan Robson, supplying the goals.

We celebrated our hard-fought victory over the Londoners by romping home 4-0 against Oxford United at Old Trafford. Mark Hughes, Steve Bruce and Bryan Robson were the scorers, along with the help of an own goal. Beardsmore and Gill came on as substitutes.

We had a tough time at Bournemouth to gain a 1-1 replay with a goal from Hughes. The fans had really got excited and there was a 52,000 gate to see Brian McClair give us a 1-0 win. Big crowds were a feature of our Cup run that season. We had had nearly 48,000 for the visit of Oxford which, with all due respect to the opposition, was a tremendous attendance.

Then everything came unstuck when we lost to Forest. You need luck in the Cup and we didn't get it. Forest fought hard but I didn't think we deserved to go out. I believe we scored a good goal which photographs later showed should have been allowed to stand. Paul McGrath put in a header which Brian McClair, in my view, forced over the line. Every Forest player stopped. They had resigned themselves to a goal and one picture showed Stuart Pearce looking to the sky in dismay as much as to say: 'Oh, no.' What was particularly disappointing was that Brian Hill, the referee, was standing virtually on the post but chose to disallow it – and that's the last time I shall ever mention his name!

The Cup run had certainly had its moments and it was to prove the feature of the season. We had Lee Sharpe in at left-back and doing quite well. Lee Martin also made his mark that season and, but for injuries, I'm sure he would now be an England full-back. Sharpe has since gone on to prove his worth but some of the other youngsters haven't made the same progress.

Tony Gill was very unlucky indeed. He would undoubtedly have made it but for a badly broken ankle. He would have become a player like Clayton Blackmore, capable of doing well in a number of positions. He had decent pace and was good in the air for his height. He had already been out for a full year with a torn Achilles tendon and up until December of that season we were really worried about him coming back at all. He was limping terribly in training but suddenly the limp vanished and he was running freely. He scored a good goal against QPR and also against Millwall. He was looking really good but then in the game at Nottingham Forest he got hit in a tackle by Brian Laws. Tony, being brave, put a foot in when it might have been wiser to let his opponent have the ball. The defender went through him and his career was finished.

Russell Beardsmore is a tremendously talented little player but lacks the strength to play at our level every week. David Wilson didn't quite have the pace to play for Manchester United and we eventually gave him a free transfer. I am sure he will enjoy a good career a step down, though. Deiniol Graham will also get a career in the game even if he didn't quite have the control I was looking for in our squad.

At least we gave our youngsters a chance. They were not forgotten. I am well aware that a lot of people thought I should have stuck with them longer. They got their chances through injury but as the senior players regained fitness I gradually replaced them. I believe I did the right thing. I was thrilled for the young ones myself but I didn't think they were quite good enough to sustain their form.

I also came under fire around this time over Ralph Milne. I signed him from Bristol City as short-term cover because I was looking for a wide player when I thought Gordon Strachan was signing for a French club. There was no great flair about him but I didn't think he was a bad signing for us. However, I learned the hard way that as far as the United supporters are concerned, if you sign any 28-year-old player for a £160,000 fee they regard him either as a cast-off or a dud. They never gave him any encouragement and it just didn't work. The club had been down that road before me as well, with the signing of players like Mark Higgins and Peter Barnes, but stop-gaps just don't have a chance at Old Trafford.

Overall I don't think it was a very lucky season for us. In addition to our controversial exit from the FA Cup at Nottingham Forest, we found ourselves caught up in a contentious match at Wimbledon and its aftermath, the infamous tunnel incident which through no fault of ours left us with a black mark. Although I said I would never mention Brian Hill's name again I have to say he was the referee in charge of that game and ask if it was his action four minutes from the end which prompted John Fashanu to behave the way he did.

What happened was that Mr Hill stopped the game and summoned a senior police officer on to the field. The rest of us were left looking at each other wondering what was going on, and I imagine the crowd were equally puzzled. It transpired that the official had asked for a police escort to be ready on the final whistle to see him safely off the pitch. No-one I know can understand why he thought it necessary to do this and at the subsequent inquest the FA in their wisdom chose to ignore the referee's unusual departure. Anyway Brian Hill duly sprinted off, never to be seen again. Despite all the mayhem to come he stayed in his room. I feel a referee like George Courtney, would have been out like a flash to see what was happening and the presence of an official would have calmed things down a lot quicker.

At the end of the match, as the referee raced off, our players went to pay their respects to our travelling support who had been very good considering we had just lost 2-1 to two goals scored by one of our former players, Terry Gibson. I waited and then we walked up the tunnel where I caught a glimpse of Viv Anderson trying to get past John Fashanu, who stood in his way as he tried to get to the dressing-rooms.

The rest of the players came tumbling in and I held them back. Eric Young, followed by Steve Bruce, were the first on to the scene as Fashanu ran up the tunnel to disappear into the home dressing-room.

All hell was let loose. Players were pulling each other about and it was one of those things you could do without. Viv was lying on the floor, unconscious. Later, after an FA inquiry, Graham Kelly, the chief executive designate, in a *Guardian* report, said that the Commission was satisfied Fashanu had hit Anderson, but that our man had 'directed insulting and improper comments' at the Wimbledon player. Fashanu was banned for three matches and fined £2,000. Viv was suspended for one game and fined £750. The sad part is that John has a bubbling personality and projects himself well on television. He does a lot of charity work which is tremendously worthy but there is another side to him. Football is a game of emotion and for some reason it appears he decided to take his feelings out on Viv Anderson that night. I asked Viv to press charges with the police because I don't think that kind of situation should be tolerated.

If it had been the old handbags at dawn that we experienced with Arsenal the following season then you would have simply said behave yourself and let it go at that. This was totally different. I had never seen anything like it in football before, which is why I called the police.

Quite frankly it proved an absolute waste of time, right up to and including the FA inquiry which turned out a complete whitewash. John Fashanu defended himself and I'll never forget his magic line when he asked the disciplinary committee: 'Look, would a Dr Barnardo's boy do something like that?'

I had to give him ten out of ten for that one! You could see the FA members nodding their heads in agreement and saying to themselves: 'Of course not, John.'

For me, the really upsetting part came later when John wrote a newspaper article trying to justify himself. He was totally out of order. There was a bit of niggle towards the end but not enough to justify what happened and Viv has had a number of libel actions settled in his favour. I have had one myself arising from the incident, which puts the whole thing in the right perspective.

I was not happy either with the part played by the FA. I remember Graham Kelly, phoning me the day after it happened, urging me to take proceedings and sort out that kind of thing once and for all. That was his attitude and I thought we were in good hands, but we ended up getting punished as well and it possibly reflects a problem Manchester United have to handle time after time.

It's as if people think we are too big for our boots, and they can't resist an opportunity to have a crack at us. We are sometimes punished for what we are, rather than for what we might have done. We are never seen to be lily-white which means we have to be ultra-careful in everything we do. I would certainly never take a case to the FA again in similar circumstances. We got our fingers burned and it taught me a lesson.

It was a bitter experience which somehow seemed to marry into an ill-fated season along with our horrendous injury list.

I have got to add that in many ways I admire the tremendous team spirit which runs through Wimbledon. They have always enjoyed knocking the big clubs for six. They are a bit like the Dead End Kids of film fame, tough but loveable, at least when it's not you they are roughing up. They want to show everyone how strong they are and in the process they knock people about. In many ways you take your hat off to their all-for-one, and one-for-all attitude, but it has to be kept within bounds if it is to be accepted. Actually it is more refined now and I don't expect we shall see the Wimbledon of three or four years ago ever again.

They were a motley crew, with players like Vinny Jones, and they used to try to frighten you as a matter of course, very often succeeding as well – and I only sit on the bench! In the FA Cup final when they shocked the football world by beating Liverpool I'm told there was an incredible atmosphere of intimidation in the tunnel as the players waited to come out at Wembley. I believe more than a few Liverpool players were shaking in their socks.

Stories abound in the football world of how they tried to foster this physical presence, of how their manager at the time, Bobby Gould, used to encourage bust-ups among the players in training to get their pent-up aggression bubbling. It's a form of tribalism with rituals and you cannot knock it altogether because it has got them where they are today, up among the big boys. As I say, they have changed somewhat now and they have better players with the introduction of people like Barton, Scales, Fitzgerald, Miller and McGhee.

John Fashanu is in fact a very underrated centre-forward. Whether his high profile would suit a big club, I'm not sure. He is certainly a personable young man, except perhaps in a tunnel. The Wimbledon style is part of football and managers like me have had to come to grips with it. We have had to find ways of handling it – not easy, as three or four successive defeats against them spelt out loud and clear.

You have to accept them for what they are. It's not my way, but they get results. You have to expect a barrage of crosses along with a cocktail of intimidation. It illustrates the variety you get in British football, which is one of its many attractions. I'm happy to say that we haven't lost since the tunnel scene and they don't upset me any more. I must admit that when they had the old crowd I was always glad to get away from the place. Now it's just another game and you see qualities you admire from players who are all fit and athletic.

But the tunnel was certainly the black spot of that season, though of course it wasn't all bad and on the credit side the return of Hughes had at least prompted a resurgence of passion among the supporters. I think also they had enjoyed the Cup run featuring the youngsters. I realised, though, that I needed to examine our strength and the FA Cup defeat at Nottingham Forest became a watershed in the affairs of Manchester United. It became my moment of decision. I had to take stock and the conclusion was that I had had enough of it.

I wanted a team capable of winning the Championship. There had been some bright moments in the League, such as the thrilling game at Liverpool when we had torn them apart to win 3-1 with goals from McClair, Hughes and Beardsmore. I was so pleased until we were coming up the tunnel at the end of the game and Ronnie Moran said to me that the best team had lost. It was a typical Ronnie Moran statement and I must admit it needled me because if there was ever a time when we had annihilated them, that was it!

The comment may even have been lurking in the back of my mind when we were knocked out of the Cup because that was the moment I decided that I was not prepared to accept Liverpool's domination of English football any longer. I resolved that I had to change everything round and gather a squad around me capable of winning the League. I just knew I had to go for it. I had been preparing by letting Peter Davenport and Jesper Olsen go, and then within hours of the Forest game Strachan was moving to Leeds.

I used the rest of the season to get some kind of form into the team while I assessed how good the young ones would become if I persevered with them. I felt Lee Sharpe had done well in his first senior season playing at left-back, and I wasn't sure which would turn out to be his best position. This was also the season of another promising winger, Jules Maiorana, a boy from the Midlands of Italian parentage who ran with his head down but at an amazing speed with an array of tricks. Later he ran into a serious knee injury which almost put him out of the game. At the time, though, he was full of potential and I gave him a couple of games as well as selecting him as a substitute in four or five games.

We ended up in 13th position while Arsenal challenged Liverpool for the Championship and won it in a head-to-head at the end of the season with that dramatic goal from Michael Thomas. I bet Kenny Dalglish has had a few nightmares about that goal since then. Television couldn't have hoped for a better drama and it was an incredible achievement for George Graham.

I looked around at my rival managers at the end of that season. Brian Clough was a kind of elder statesman, a boss who had done virtually everything from the League title to success in Europe. Then there was my age group or slightly younger, like Howard Kendall and Terry Venables with Kenny Dalglish and George Graham, two Scots competing for the final Championship honours.

I realised it was all about beating Dalglish and Graham, fellow Scots, and I had this gut feeling that if I didn't have a go I wasn't going to make it as a soccer boss this side of the border. George had challenged the might of Anfield and come out on top. He had built a resourceful club and it was maybe his winning of the League title which gave me the impetus I needed. I resolved there and then that if he could do it so could I.

At one of the board meetings towards the end of the season the directors agreed that I had shown a willingness to part with players in an effort to contribute towards getting expensive new ones in. So they gave me the go-ahead to build a stronger team and I looked around at the players available.

I had tried for Neil Webb a couple of years previously – to no avail – but he was now at the end of his contract and seemed to be ready to listen to offers. I was attracted because he was skilful, a tremendous passer of the ball and, though a midfielder, had been averaging a dozen goals a season. I was beginning to appreciate that Bryan Robson would have to be replaced some time and so there was also room for another midfield player.

Les Kershaw had decided to watch Paul Ince in every game in the closing stages of the season and every time he came back he waxed lyrical about the boy's potential and his competitive streak. He said that although he needed a bit of work, we must get him. It was one of those positive recommendations you like from a chief scout at times like that, and we set the wheels in motion.

We also liked the look of Mike Phelan at Norwich, an unsung hero but a player who got everywhere on the pitch. He could play in a few different positions and was a good reader of the game. Although we were now in for three midfield players I told the directors we may as well take them all because there were very few players available. They backed me and I think it proved a wise decision because it was that summer that we agreed it would be better for both Paul McGrath and Norman Whiteside to continue their careers elsewhere. It was a major decision but at least it broke the deadlock.

It's never easy getting a player off Brian Clough. I thought at one time that I was going to be able to sign Stuart Pearce after he had let it be known that he was interested in coming to Old Trafford, but at the end of the day he signed a new contract with Forest. With hindsight it was probably the best thing for him. He is a fine full-back, but he likes the quiet life, very seldom gives interviews and is better suited to a club like Nottingham Forest.

Neil Webb, on the other hand, was a different cup of tea, more flamboyant, more worldly and with the kind of profile to fit in at Old Trafford. I felt that even Brian Clough wouldn't be able to dodge the transfer this time because Neil was coming out of contract and was therefore available. Even so, the first time I went to the City Ground and asked to see Brian, the secretary came back to say he wasn't in ... despite the fact that his car was parked outside as large as life!

That is all part of the Clough style of course. He likes to tease you and create an air of mystique. He likes to baffle, even to the point of eccentricity. Earlier in the season I went to a reserve game there at his invitation but we couldn't agree a deal. Come the summer though, it was a different ball game. Neil was out of contract and free to negotiate. We didn't have to play hide and seek with Brian and the transfer went through very quickly.

Brian never takes a phone call direct. He makes even his fellow managers go through his assistant, Ron Fenton, and he is quite a complicated man. It's never easy to have a conversation with him and he has these swings of mood, but he has great bouts of generosity and kindness. He has helped a lot of people. I certainly don't look on him as an ogre, more the elder statesman of managers in the game at the moment, and I think it is true to say that he commands a great deal of respect from the rest of us.

You don't get tradition easily in our game. It can take 20 years or more. Brian Clough has established his style and that is to play football in the real meaning of the word. Everyone in the game admires that and, regardless of what you might think of the man himself, his eccentricity is more than compensated for by the fun of his team.

So we got Webb in the bag and then we ran into problems trying to negotiate with West Ham for Paul Ince. The club had just sacked John Lyall and were in the throes of appointing a new manager. Their Chairman couldn't give us a decision until the new man was in the chair, which clinched the decision to go for Mike Phelan. His contract was up at Norwich and it was a pleasure to do business with Robert Chase, their Chairman. They wanted £800,000, we offered £700,000, and so we split the difference and paid £750,000 without the hassle of going to a League tribunal.

Then, around this time, we went for one that got away!

The agent and lawyer for Glenn Hysen telephoned to say that the Swedish international centre-half was desperate to join us after coming to the end of his contract with Fiorentina. We were told there wouldn't be a big price on his head. We contacted an English representative and a deal was put in motion for a figure of around £300,000. I spoke to the player and then went on holiday to leave the Chairman to entertain the player and his party on a visit to Old Trafford. Martin Edwards could not have done more in staging a big reception. Bobby Charlton was there and so was Bryan Robson, who took Hysen to his home. Terms were agreed and it was left to us to speak to Fiorentina to finalise the fee.

The Chairman asked what I would think if the fee started to drift up to £500,000, as so often happens. I replied that on top of his substantial personal terms it would be too much for a player who was nearly 30. The Chairman had got the right vibes because Fiorentina then started to push the fee to £600,000 plus playing a game for them in Italy.

It started to drag and while we hesitated over the escalating fee Liverpool slipped in the back door and agreed the club's fee. Full marks to them, but Fiorentina might have told us before we flew out to Milan to try and conclude the transfer. As soon as I saw Liverpool at the airport I knew we had competition.

Liverpool were the first to talk to Hysen and at that point his agent told us his man had signed for Liverpool three days previously. I asked him how he could go back on his word after shaking hands on it with us in Manchester and not even have the decency to tell us before dragging us out to Italy.

My anger told him what I thought of him and my conclusion was that after going back on his word we didn't want Hysen anyway. Somewhere along the line it has turned out to be a blessing in disguise because it forced us to go the whole hog for Gary Pallister.

We got a lot of adverse publicity at the time. People thought we had been slow but in fact Liverpool did us a big favour. It must have cost them more than £1.25 million for him over two years and they never got a penny back. Then they had to buy Mark Wright as a replacement for £2.1 million. It adds up to over £3 million for their centre-half position, which makes Pallister at £2.3 million look a bargain. At the time it looked as if Liverpool had put one over on us, but in the long term we have come out better.

Anyway, as soon as the Hysen deal had fallen down I phoned Bruce Rioch for Pallister. After two or three weeks' negotiating we still hadn't settled anything and we were coming to the start of the season. Bruce is not easy to deal with and the Middlesbrough Chairman, Colin Henderson, must be the hardest man in Britain. He is a top executive of ICI and it showed. He couldn't have driven a harder bargain.

We eventually arranged to meet them and drove up with Maurice Watkins, our director and the club solicitor. He asked what I thought should be the top limit we should pay. I said we should offer £1.3 million and perhaps be prepared to go to around £1.8 million, though I was well aware that for the sake of their supporters they would probably want to reach the magic figure of £2 million.

The evening started very pleasantly but with their Chairman saying from the outset: 'We want £2.3 million or you can forget it'. The battle started and we were in and out of the room like a fiddler's elbow. In one of the interludes Maurice asked me if I really wanted him and of course I assured him he was vital to my plans. We finished six hours later, agreeing to the fee originally demanded by their Chairman.

It had been a long day and we began to consider how we were going to break the news of the fee to our Chairman who had missed everything because he was away in Spain on holiday. 'What a lovely wake-up call we have for him,' I told Maurice, 'but rather you than me to make it!' So concluded the saga of Gary Pallister, a record fee for us but one I don't regret paying.

He has emerged well. In the early days he was like a new-born foal. He had no real physique about him apart from his height. Now he is much stronger and we still haven't seen the best of him. He will get better and better. He has had some tremendous games for us and eventually he will be captain material.

I have got to say that he got off to a sloppy start but it was always going to be difficult signing so many players at the same time. I knew, though, that I had to rebuild, no matter the immediate difficulties, and I also tried to buy Trevor Steven.

I was unbelievably disappointed in him. When he came to Old Trafford he had no enthusiasm for the club, and out of all the players I have negotiated with, Trevor was the only one who didn't want to look around the stadium, see the pitch and get the feel of the place. The only thing his wife seemed concerned about was whether we had a nursery for her kids. I was flat after speaking to him and I can only think that the Rangers offer had already turned him off us.

Our terms were good, though I concede they didn't match the Ibrox offer. At the same time you would think that giving someone the chance to come to Old Trafford would at least prompt an enthusiastic response. I didn't get it from Trevor Steven though, and I said to our Chairman that he was no use to us with that kind of attitude. It was still a disappointment because he would have given us a nice balance on the right side to replace Strachan.

It left me still looking for a wide player, though there was the young Lee Sharpe to consider. At that point, though, I wasn't sure whether he was going to be a winger or a left-back. So I concluded it might be better to get someone who could play on both flanks and Danny Wallace fitted the bill. I reached a deal with Southampton for £1.2 million and signed him without any real difficulty.

He was keen to play for us and brought a little buzz to the place, though I think Danny would be the first to admit that Old Trafford has been a little bit big for him. I know that he will go away and give someone great service, which is why Southampton tried to buy him back.

So now we come to the last piece of the five-man rebuilding, and Paul Ince proved the most traumatic of the lot. Les Kershaw raved about the lad and I saw him as a basic raw talent with an instinct to win, two good feet, courage and the possibility that he could develop into a Bryan Robson type. He had scored nine goals for West Ham that season and though his scoring has deserted him since, I believe it will come again as he grows into Manchester United.

The first difficulty arose when Paul was persuaded to wear a United shirt for a picture in one of the newspapers before he had actually signed for us. If you know Lou Macari and consider the pride of West Ham it was the worst thing he could have done. It caused us embarrassment because at that point we had not even spoken to the player. Lou came round when he realised that Paul only wanted to play for us and the player came to Manchester with his agent, Ambrose Mendy, who pleasantly surprised me.

He handled the transfer far better than a lot of agents I have dealt with and was prepared to come middle of the road in a lot of things. The tactics with so many agents these days is to ask for everything, money for goals, bonuses for winning on top of normal bonuses, a certain make of car, a particular type of house in a special kind of road. They come with a list as long as your arm, oblivious to the fact that you are already paying them for the things they itemise. Ambrose Mendy was fair-minded and the transfer went brilliantly until we reached the medical stage.

Off Paul went with Jim McGregor, our physiotherapist, for x-rays and the rest, mentioning along the way that he had been bothered by a pelvic problem. This was the first we had heard about it. Naturally Jim asked for more extensive investigation and further x-rays showed some deviance. We felt he should see a specialist because £1.5 million is a lot of money if there is something likely to go wrong. The transfer came to a full stop.

The boy took it badly; we all took it badly. Ambrose and Clare, now his wife, were shocked and it left us all in a limbo. I said we had better speak to West Ham, particularly as it was obviously going to

More champagne as Manager of the Month for the fifth time

My first squad after becoming manager of Manchester United:
Back Row: *Nicky Wood, Lee Martin, Steve Bruce, Viv Anderson, Peter Davenport, Paul McGrath, Liam O'Brien, Norman Whiteside*
Middle: *Archie Knox (coach), me, Clayton Blackmore, Chris Turner, Jim Leighton, Gary Walsh, Billy Garton, Jim McGregor (physiotherapist), Norman Davies (kit manager)*
Front: *Kevin Moran, Mike Duxbury, Jesper Olsen, Mark Hughes, Bryan Robson, Brian McClair, Gordon Strachan, Colin Gibson*

Paul McGrath ... I had to transfer him for his own good. We were on a collision course

Gordon Strachan said I lost faith in him

I can still be a goalmouth nuisance! Playing for United against Somerset Cricket Club during the 1987 tour of Bermuda

My first trophy for Manchester United, the FA Cup and a life-saver!

Sir Matt Busby, President of Manchester United, meets the new goalkeeper, Peter Schmeichel, at his long overdue testimonial match

Racing into the future ... Nicky Butt, Colin McKee and David Beckham celebrate a semi-final victory at Tottenham on their way to winning the FA Youth Cup of 1992

Bryan Robson is in my team for next season and how we could have done with him in the closing weeks of the last Championship challenge. He would have steadied the ship

I can still manage a trick or two with the ball

Still proud to wear a Scotland jersey

We had to give young Ryan Giggs a new contract so that he could take delivery of a club car like the rest of the players in the first team

be difficult for Paul to play for them again. The supporters would have slaughtered him. Ambrose asked if we would mind if they got their own specialist to look at Paul and I told him to go ahead. We needed a projection of the injury and we all got our heads together.

We decided that the fair way would be to pay £500,000 down with the other £1 million based on appearances. As we all know now, everything has turned out well. He has had a couple of ankle injuries, a knee, a calf strain but only the run of the mill injuries every player gets. In fact to show our appreciation of the way they conducted the transfer, we later waived the payment clause and we gave West Ham the rest of the money last season so that they could buy Clive Allen to help in their battle against relegation. Paul was also given a new contract and he is emerging as a player of standing at the club, likeable, volatile and a personality who is starting to take his character out on to the park. He is still only 24 and I feel we shall see him emerge as a top Manchester United player over the next few years.

The big five signings cost a total of £7.3 million, a lot of money which brought my total spending with the club to around £12 million. Some of it has been offset by selling players of course. Nevertheless, the media have latched on to this idea that I am a big-spending manager, but you have to put it in perspective. You have to consider the revenue of Manchester United, the status of the club and the demands of the supporters who regularly give us the biggest gates in the country.

Frankly, I consider I have done very well with my spending. I don't think anyone should criticise it. I certainly don't like this idea of moneybags Fergie, particularly as I have always worked hard at establishing a successful youth policy. Where our weakness lies is that we don't seem able to sell at the level of other big clubs like, say, Liverpool, who last season were able to sell Steve McMahon at the age of 31 for nearly £1 million. That was very good business for them and I wish we could do more deals like that. We are expected to give our players away, which is why I am never in a hurry to sell players who are invariably reluctant to leave anyway. It's also something that has got to change.

From the playing point of view, I was delighted with the additional talent, though I had to recognise problems arising from doing that amount of business all at once. The weakness was having too many players all trying to adjust at the same time and living in hotels for weeks on end. It was particularly difficult for Danny Wallace with a young family. Then of course they all had to adjust to playing for Manchester United on probably the most demanding stage of all.

They had all come from different kinds of backgrounds and smaller clubs – Southampton, a homely south coast team, Norwich, with its country set-up, West Ham, one of the smaller London sides, Middlesbrough, in the Second Division, and Nottingham Forest, with its special Brian Clough culture.

You try to do your homework and go for players who will settle quickly, but with hindsight I was perhaps a manager in too much of a hurry and over-ambitious.

SEASON 1988-89
First Division

	P	W	D	L	F	A	PTS
Arsenal	38	22	10	6	73	36	76
Liverpool	38	22	10	6	65	28	76
Nottingham Forest	38	17	13	8	64	43	64
Norwich City	38	17	11	10	48	45	62
Derby County	38	17	7	14	40	38	58
Tottenham Hotspur	38	15	12	11	60	46	57
Coventry City	38	14	13	11	47	42	55
Everton	38	14	12	12	50	45	54
Queens Park Rangers	38	14	11	13	43	37	53
Millwall	38	14	11	13	47	52	53
MANCHESTER UNITED	38	13	12	13	45	35	51
Wimbledon	38	14	9	15	50	46	51
Southampton	38	10	15	13	52	66	45
Charlton Athletic	38	10	12	16	44	58	42
Sheffield Wednesday	38	10	12	16	34	51	42
Luton Town	38	10	11	17	42	52	40
Aston Villa	38	9	13	16	45	56	40
Middlesbrough	38	9	12	17	44	61	39
West Ham United	38	10	8	20	37	62	38
Newcastle United	38	7	10	21	32	63	31

APPEARANCES

	League	Littlewoods Cup	FA Cup	Total
Steve Bruce	38	3	7	48
Mark Hughes	38	3	7	48
Jim Leighton	38	3	7	48
Brian McClair	38	3	7	48
Bryan Robson	34	3	6	43
Mal Donaghy	30	0	7	37
Clayton Blackmore	26(2)	3	5(1)	34(3)
Gordon Strachan	21	2(1)	5	28(1)
Lee Sharpe	19(3)	2	5(1)	26(4)
Ralph Milne	19(3)	0	7	26(3)
Lee Martin	20(4)	0	4(1)	24(5)
Paul McGrath	18(2)	1	4(1)	23(3)
Russell Beardsmore	17(6)	1(1)	3(2)	21(9)
Mike Duxbury	16(2)	3	0	19(2)
Billy Garton	13(1)	2	0	15(1)
Peter Davenport	7(1)	1(1)	0	8(2)
Jesper Olsen	6(4)	1(1)	0	7(5)
Tony Gill	4(5)	0	2(2)	6(7)
Norman Whiteside	6	0	0	6
Viv Anderson	5(1)	0(1)	0	5(2)
Mark Robins	1(8)	0(1)	1	2(9)
Giuliano Maiorana	2(4)	0	0	2(4)
Liam O'Brien	1(2)	1	0	2(2)
Colin Gibson	1(1)	1	0	2(1)
David Wilson	0(4)	0	0(2)	0(6)
Derek Brazil	0(1)	0	0	0(1)
Deiniol Graham	0	0	0(1)	0(1)

GOALSCORERS

	League	Littlewoods Cup	FA Cup	Total
Mark Hughes	14	0	2	16
Brian McClair	10	3	3 (inc 1 pen)	16 (inc 1 pen)
Bryan Robson	4	2	2	8
Steve Bruce	2	1	1	4
Peter Davenport	2	1	1	4
Clayton Blackmore	3	0	0	3
Ralph Milne	3	0	0	3
Russell Beardsmore	2	0	0	2
Tony Gill	1	0	1	2
Deiniol Graham	0	0	1	1
Lee Martin	1	0	0	1
Paul McGrath	1	0	0	1
Gordon Strachan	1	0	0	1
Own Goals	1	0	1	2
Total	45	7	11 (inc 1 pen)	64 (inc 1 pen)

FA CUP

Round 3	QPR	(H)	D	0-0
Replay	QPR	(A)	D	2-2 aet
Replay	QPR	(H)	W	3-0
Round 4	Oxford	(H)	W	4-0
Round 5	Bournemouth	(A)	D	1-1
Replay	Bournemouth	(H)	W	1-0
Round 6	Nottingham F.	(H)	L	0-1

LEAGUE CUP

Round 2/1	Rotheram U.	(A)	W	1-0
Round 2/2	Rotheram U.	(H)	W	5-0
Round 3	Wimbledon	(A)	L	1-2

Chapter Five

ET TU, BRUTE

The knives were out and for a period it seemed I might become yet another statistic in the pursuit of success at Old Trafford. I certainly see season 1989-90 as the watershed of my career with Manchester United. The problem was that my £7 million summer splash in the transfer market caused hardly a ripple in terms of our League football.

Four defeats in the first seven games was a dud start and a mid-season spell of 11 games without a win had my critics busy sharpening those blades. But the FA Cup came to my rescue, starting with a morale-boosting third round win at Nottingham Forest and going through to victory in the final against Crystal Palace.

The Cup proved my life-saver, but for someone else at Old Trafford it sounded a career death knell. I had good cause to thank my lucky stars for the glamour and glory of Wembley; not so, unlucky Jim Leighton who to this very day must still be cursing the English FA Cup.

I dropped Jim for the final replay and while I did not do it lightly, I never anticipated the blight I was putting on his life. As one of the newspapers describing my team selection for the second game against Palace put it: 'Et tu, Brute.'

That stabbed home like the knives that only a few weeks earlier were being prepared for me and I have got to say that if I could have my time over again I would not have dropped Jim Leighton ... not because it was wrong from the football point of view but because it wrecked his career and cost him two years of his footballing life. You must remember that Jim was a goalkeeper I had nurtured as a boy. I gave him his debut at Aberdeen and we had come a long way together.

At the start of the season, after strengthening the squad, I thought we were in for a good run. We certainly opened well enough by beating Arsenal 4–1, a match highlighted by Michael Knighton coming out before the kick-off to do his ball-juggling act. On the morning of the match, the Chairman asked me to come and see him. He explained he had sold the club to Knighton who had offered to build a new Stretford End stand. I think Martin Edwards also felt he had done as much as he could to please the supporters. I was quite surprised, though of course I knew about the background saga. Now the Chairman was telling me that a deal had been struck and Michael was next-door waiting to meet me.

He was very pleasant and he assured me that I would get his total backing and that things would carry on more or less as before. It was agreed that I would introduce him to the staff. It was at that point I wished I had been a former Manchester United player because when I presented my assistants like Archie Knox, Eric Harrison and Jim McGregor, he stood back and said how tremendous it was to meet two legends like Brian Kidd and Nobby Stiles.

They were duly embarrassed, but it was nothing to the stick they got after Michael had left. Everybody teased them that obviously they would be OK under the next regime. No-one will forget that first day when Michael went out on to the pitch, dressed in United strip. I tried to talk him out of it. I told him the Press would crucify him but he ignored all advice because he genuinely wanted to show he was one of the real supporters. It was done with his best intentions but the aftermath was something we could have done without. It's now part of the folklore of the club. So many controversial things happen at Old Trafford, things you wish had not happened and it's manna for the Press. It makes headlines and embarrasses us.

Michael's curtain-raiser didn't do us any harm on the day. We were flying against Arsenal, with goals from Steve Bruce, Neil Webb, Brian McClair and Mark Hughes. Our opening team lined up: Leighton, Duxbury, Blackmore, Bruce, Phelan, Donaghy, Robson, Webb, McClair, Hughes, Sharpe. Subs: Martin, Robins.

We also slaughtered Crystal Palace away in the next match though Ian Wright scored in the last minute to send us away with only a 1–1 draw.

It was a dampener and we needed to get our game together. However, we lost the next three matches before suddenly bursting into life with a 5-1 win against Millwall featuring a hat-trick from Mark Hughes.

But it was an up and down season because the very next League match brought one of the worst days of my career with a 5-1 defeat against Manchester City at Maine Road. What stands out in my mind was that Jim Leighton hardly had a save to make in the game. City got four corners to our 12 and we were doing well until there was crowd trouble in the Kippax Stand and the teams were taken off the pitch. They came back out and City scored two in five minutes. We were struck dumb. We had some good chances and we had a couple cleared off the line. Cooper made a good save from Mark Hughes but the fact is we came in three down.

It has to be said that, defensively, we were poor but we again started well in the second half and got back to 3-1 before David White scored with a marvellous piece of work after the ball had cannoned off the referee. So it ended 5-1 and the cameras were around the dugout as if they were filming an obituary, which they nearly were.

I remember going home. It had been an early kick-off and I was back at the house for 3 p.m. I went straight to my bed and put my head under the pillow. Cathy came in and asked what had happened. I could hardly answer. I was in total shock and completely gone.

But you have to recover from these things. We had a good performance at Coventry and then we hit a dreadful spell which cast doubts over my future and destroyed a lot of the players' confidence. In mitigation, we had horrendous injury problems and what I can't understand is that in that kind of situation other clubs like Liverpool get sympathy. Not us though, and the only solace is that it proves how big a club we are and that we are expected to rise above mundane problems such as injuries.

Still, we managed a terrific performance at Luton where we won 3-1 but then towards the end of November we went 11 games in a row without a League win. We drew five and lost six. Wedged in between was our FA Cup victory in the third round at Nottingham Forest which many people identify as the turning point in the career of Alex Ferguson at Old Trafford and his future as manager of Manchester United.

Before the Cup-tie was certainly the blackest period in my life as a manager, because in analysing the games I have to say we actually played quite well without being able to win. We had too many draws. The darkest day was undoubtedly at home to Crystal Palace when I left out Mark Hughes and the crowd were not slow to voice their objections to what was clearly an unpopular decision on my part.

I brought him on as a substitute a few minutes after the interval but it didn't do any good and we lost 2-1. I will never forget going home with the draw for the third round of the FA Cup to be made. I listened in horror as we drew Nottingham Forest away. What a day! The great thing about the Forest tie, as it turned out, was not so much the win, but the defiance of our support. They never stopped cheering the whole afternoon. Everybody was smelling defeat for us. Jimmy Hill even said we looked like a beaten team in the warm-up. On reflection, I bet many people can't remember my team that day. It read: Leighton, Anderson, Bruce, Pallister, Martin, Blackmore, McClair, Phelan, Beardsmore, Robins, Hughes. Subs: Duxbury, Milne.

I mention it because it was an illustration of the injuries we had at that time. One of the most encouraging aspects was that all the injured regulars out of the team went down with us for the match. We had Webb, Robson, Ince, Donaghy, Wallace and Sharpe all sitting in the stands. But the lads I picked performed magnificently. They worked themselves into the ground and got a deserved 1-0 win with a goal scored by Mark Robins, bless him. Forest had a goal chalked off near the end but it was a foul on Jim Leighton and it was offside as well. It was an inspired performance for the supporters and myself. It was a happy dressing-room and you could sense the players and directors were happy for me after all the speculation about my future following our rough ride in the League.

The nice touch had been that the Chairman had called me up to his office the day before the match. We were in the midst of a crisis and the Press had been badgering him for a statement about my future. They wanted him to give me a vote of confidence before the Cup-tie and they hoped he would say that if we lost I would be sacked. The media had been working hard at creating pressure and they wanted Martin Edwards to respond to the speculation.

I have to acknowledge that the Chairman and the board were brilliant. Never once in all my time at the club have they questioned the details of my management or asked in what direction I was heading. They trusted me and supported me in all my decisions concerning the buying of new players and those leaving, like Strachan and Davenport, Whiteside and McGrath. They knew my policies were right and that my work revitalising the youth set-up had been important.

In my moment of crisis the Chairman told me that he didn't think the board should come out publicly and say they were supporting me because that kind of vote of confidence so often turns out to be a kiss of death. Martin Edwards said the papers would use it to their own advantage. He added that what he would tell me privately was that even if we lost the Cup-tie I would not be sacked.

I found it tremendously encouraging and I know he meant it. You can imagine that, apart from my own feelings, I was also happy for the people around me, my staff who had been working so hard. You have got to understand the psychology of the Press in the kind of situation I found myself. It's always good copy if Manchester United are sacking their manager and if you are not actually winning something they want the other side of the coin and the manager dismissed. The media have little time for anything but the extremes of black and white. An average performance just does not make a good story. If you are not pulling in trophies then they whittle away at your confidence with speculation about the future. Then the whole business of the next appointment starts all over again. It's a game called selling newspapers.

A manager who wishes to retain his sanity has to shut it out of his mind. You have to reject all these media hypes and manage the club as you see it. Of all the bits of advice Sir Matt Busby has given me, one of the best was his counsel when things are not going too well: 'Don't buy the papers and certainly don't read them.' For a man in the autumn of his years he comes up with gems of advice worth thinking about. For when you are under pressure you start worrying about not only your future but that of the staff. You think, if I go then the coaching staff might go as well. You have a concern for them because you pick them, people like Nobby Stiles and Brian Kidd, old heroes at the club.

When the going gets tough the staff look to you for a lead. The players also want to be helped. The frustrating thing was that I felt we were close to getting it right, as the Cup run later showed. Then on the heels of all the depression came the Forest tie. The response in the dressing-room was fantastic. There was a real sense of purpose and determination, not only to win that match but to go all the way in the competition.

Minutes after the match we heard we had been drawn away at Hereford in the fourth round so there was a lot of optimism in the dressing-room. In the run-up to the game we had brought Les Sealey to the club from Luton reserves as cover for Jim Leighton. He was as excited as a kid with the result. He had involved himself with our fortunes right from the start. He's a volatile, irascible man of many contradictory moods. You just didn't know what was going to happen where he was concerned. You had to bend to his eccentric behaviour at times and laugh at it because that was his nature. When he and Paul Ince, two Cockneys, used to get going with the banter no-one knew what they were on about. They were worse than me and Kenny Dalglish to understand.

So the next round took us to little Hereford. Steve Bruce missed the game but Mal Donaghy and Danny Wallace were back. Mike Duxbury played in the middle of the park and was star man. It was a nervous occasion and a lot of people thought the tie had the makings of a Cup upset. The pitch was a mudheap. Who could forget the car park? So much for parking early because when the fans came out they found their cars under water.

It was an edgy performance and we didn't score until late on with a great move down the right-hand side which ended with a goal for Clayton Blackmore. It got us into a memorable tie up at Newcastle, one of those games you never forget. It ebbed and flowed. They started brightly but we scored off a corner through Mark Robins and at half-time we were leading 1-0. I thought we were just getting to grips with it but the second half was a real ding-donger. They equalised with a penalty kick, but Danny Wallace scored to make it 2-1. Newcastle made it 2-2 when Jim Leighton was blatantly obstructed and you wondered if fortune was turning against you.

Paul Ince came on as a substitute and with his first touch he put Danny Wallace away for Brian McClair to grab a winner and put us through to the quarter-finals. It was a game absolutely on a knife's edge but we made it to meet Sheffield United away, a game we won far more comfortably than the score of 1-0 suggested. The team were starting to get more confident and McClair got a good goal.

Then it was into another memorable experience in the semi-finals against Oldham. The great thing about that run was the number of good games. I remember after the Hereford match, their manager, Ian Bowyer, came up and said he was really glad for me. He explained he considered it more important for me to win than for him. So there is a bit of humanity in the game and Ian is a genuine lad.

How you describe the Oldham games, I don't really know. If you had to put ten things down about what makes a good game of football, you saw them all in the 3-3 tie after extra-time at Maine Road. The big question was what did *not* happen. It had everything except a penalty kick and there should have been one of those when Neil Webb was fouled but Joe Worrall decided not to give it.

Talk about a nerve-jangler – that's when I started visibly to age. We took a risk that day by playing Bryan Robson, Neil Webb and Colin Gibson after long-term injuries to leave Danny Wallace and Mark Robins on the bench. At times we were a bit lucky, at moments unlucky. The game was well controlled. The support was mixed up together but there was no trouble. We had the replay three days later. It was just as tense but we tightened up and just about edged it. I particularly remember when we were 2-1 up and they switched to one at the back with their centre-half pushed up to centre-forward. It was a fantastic game, a great credit to both sides, but we held out.

I felt sorry for Joe Royle and on the morning of their League Cup final I 'phoned him up. I couldn't get him and spoke to his Chairman, Ian Stott, and said I hoped they would win. It was a measure of my sympathy for them going out against us in the FA Cup.

So on to Wembley to our final, and a point in your life when you wish you didn't need a certain result. The first game against Crystal Palace was one of incredible excitement with a 3-3 draw after extra-time. I thought we were a far better team. The big talking point was not the possibility of Robson holding the FA Cup aloft for the third time as our captain. It wasn't about bringing Ian Wright on as a substitute for Palace to go 3-2 up or even Mark Hughes grabbing an equaliser to give us a replay. It was undoubtedly my decision to leave Jim Leighton out of the second game.

To understand it you have to place this in a dramatic chain of consequences. I think criticism was levelled at me because people thought I was ruthless leaving out a player I had known as a lad with Aberdeen. I had launched him into international football with Scotland and had never dropped him until this Cup final replay. People recognised that as a distasteful illustration of sheer callousness.

But the scenario of it is that we won the Cup and the other incredible aspect is that the critics ignored the build-up. The people who criticised leaving him out were mostly the ones who had been getting at him in the games leading up to the final. The poor lad was taking a buffeting from supporters which he has since said he used to get during the warm-up before matches. He reckons he was never accepted by Old Trafford fans. I don't believe that, but he maintains that they were always giving him stick.

It's true that in the run-up to the Cup final that year he showed incredible nervousness. There was a constant debate between Archie Knox and myself about what we should do. We rested him a couple of times and allowed Les Sealey a chance. Les had in fact played against Aston Villa, a match we won 2-0 and against QPR, which we won 2-1.

It all boiled down to the fact that Jim had not been playing well. The semi-final brought us to the point of wondering whether to leave him out or let him see it through. We went through the scenario a host of times and I think we made the right decision to leave him in for the semi-final replay. He had a good game and we tried our best to buck up his confidence. We had a couple of chats and in one particular dressing-room discussion I told him he was the best goalkeeper Scotland had had in 30 years and it was time he started showing it.

I said to him: 'You have got the determination, now go and demonstrate you are the best keeper Scotland have ever had.' We tried that approach to get him out of himself because he is a type who tends to feel sorry for himself if things are not going right. He's a nice boy, very sensitive and possibly therein lies the problem, a situation exposed when he came to Manchester United, as it is for many who join the club. It's doubly hard for someone as sensitive as Jim Leighton if he hits a bad spell. At Aberdeen he had been protected by the success of the team, two tremendous centre-backs in front of him and his own resulting confidence.

But then, having done well in the semi-final second game, we went to Nottingham Forest where Jim had four goals put past him in the first 20 minutes. The doubts started all over again. There was a lot of discussion between Archie and myself which, for obvious reasons, we kept to ourselves.

Then we approached a home match against Charlton and I felt we must play our Cup final team. It was the last game of the season at Old Trafford and an opportunity for the fans to give the players a send-off for Wembley. The big question was – do I leave Jim out? – and it was fermenting, brewing away in my mind. Wembley can be a killer of a place for a player tormented by doubts. As a Scot, I know all about the Wembley reputation. A Cup final on a hot day can diminish the stoutest of hearts. It's a place where men of substance step forward to be counted; on the other hand it can be a hell which finds out a lot of people.

After much deliberation we decided to play him against Charlton and that he would be in the final team. It turned out he had little to do in the League game. They were booked for relegation and we won comfortably. So we went into the showdown with Crystal Palace and I soon had other things to think about. What I hadn't expected was the surprise Steve Coppell had up his sleeve for us. He had his team man-mark everybody with just one player up front which made life difficult for us. We overcame that but just as we looked to be in command they brought on Ian Wright who almost single-handedly carried them from a losing position to a winning one.

It finished a real battle which we got through with a final score of 3-3 for a replay, but at the end of the game, as we were trooping off the field, I looked at Jim Leighton and I knew he was a beaten man. In the dressing-room he sat with his head between his knees and it was then I knew he had to be left out of the replay. But how do you give a player that kind of decision, knowing how sensitive he is and how long I had known him?

People must recognise that I am not the three-headed monster that I have been portrayed. I've got feelings just like everyone else –

like Jim Leighton, in fact. I lay awake almost all night pondering whether I was doing the right thing but I kept coming back to the conclusion that the lad was struggling with his confidence.

We went down to London again for the second game and the night before the match Jim was having a game of cards with some of the other lads in the hotel. I watched them play for a while. The others went upstairs and I called Jim back to the lounge to break the news to him. He perhaps half-expected it. His reaction was to say it served him right because he knew he had played badly.

The next day he was totally dejected. I really felt for him but I had made the decision and I had to stand by it because Alex Ferguson's feelings come second to the needs of Manchester United. Over the years I have picked many teams. Some of the players I have liked and some have not really been my cup of tea. It's irrelevant because a manager is expected to make the right decisions for the club and for the supporters.

I think I got it right this time – though not for my reputation with Jim Leighton, which has suffered. I had letters from Scotland calling me a traitor and it doesn't help you get over it. I have got to say that if I had known the reaction, how much it would affect Jim, I could not have made the same decision again. With hindsight it has not been fair, either to Jim or to me.

The Press, of course, loved every minute of it, especially the 'Et tu, Brute' headline!

The rest is now history. Jim's career went for a dive. We tried to help him and eventually sold him for £150,000 to Dundee, a giveaway fee. What disappoints me about football is that after he had been pilloried by the media and he was in the stocks no-one was prepared to take his head out. The whole of the game said they were not going to handle it, they were not going to be the mug to take him after Manchester United had rejected him.

Basically he was still a top-class goalkeeper and all he needed was a fresh start somewhere else away from Old Trafford. Arsenal did him a great turn by taking him on loan for a while and he also went to Reading which helped him. But it was two years of his life wasted. Sadly, there is no way I could even begin to apologise to him because I don't think an apology is needed. I have tremendous regret but you can't apologise for doing something that needed to be done. Therein lies what Manchester United is all about. It's bigger than Alex Ferguson and Jim Leighton. It's about an incredible support which spends fortunes following the team. When they go to Wembley they deserve success and they are entitled to have a manager selecting what, in his mind, he believes to be the right team. But it won't change things between Jim and me. He has no respect for me at all, which is down to his sensitivity. His wife shunned me at the reception after we had won the Cup.

Ironically, he could play for years yet. He's a dedicated trainer and I kept telling managers he was far from finished. Alan Hodgkinson, our experienced specialist goalkeeper coach, also went out of his way to tell people in the game that Jim still had all the right qualities and that the problem had simply been one of a temporary loss of confidence.

The managers hadn't listened and, to compound it all, he had a bad experience when Scotland stood by him and took him to the World Cup. I tried to help him with the Scottish Press and asked Alex Cameron to get the writers together before Scotland set off so that Jim could talk about his disappointment and get it off his chest before concentrating on his international career again. Jim was bitter by then though, and rejected the idea. He sold his story to the *Sun* newspaper and by doing so he antagonised the rest of the Scottish papers.

He played against Brazil and lost a goal which he was widely blamed for. The only criticism I have is for the way he blamed himself. He got up after the ball had gone in and was clearly angry with himself. Most keepers would have been out of goal like a flash, blaming their defence. He certainly had every right because it was a hard shot after the Brazilians had been allowed to walk through the Scottish defence without a tackle. Jim is too honest and it was a sorry climax to a terrible summer. It ended up that I lost a player and, what I found even more disturbing, I lost his respect.

But just as it was sad for Jim Leighton, the bottom line was that we beat Crystal Palace 1-0 in the replay. We won the FA Cup for the seventh time in the club's history, with Bryan Robson holding the trophy aloft for the third time as captain. He played his part in his usual way by scoring a typical goal in the first game.

Ironically, the boy who scored in the replay to win the Cup almost didn't play. Lee Martin had been bothered by bits of cramp in a few games and I was worried about him lasting if the replay went to extra-time. So, on the morning of the match, I sought him out and tried to get a reaction. I put my concern to him, looking for a response of confident defiance which is exactly what I got. 'I'll be all right,' he said. The boy picked himself up and became a hero, little knowing how close he had been to being left out along with Jim Leighton. He was fortunate that day but he has had atrocious luck ever since. He hurt his back the following pre-season to let Clayton Blackmore in at left-back for probably his best season at the club. Later he found Denis Irwin performing miracles. Free of injuries, I think by now he would have been playing for England. Perhaps he still will because he has age on his side.

Leighton's misfortune was, of course, Les Sealey's big break. With Gary Walsh out of action we had had one or two keepers on loan as cover. They included Mark Crossley from Nottingham Forest, a player we got by way of apology from Brian Clough, who had slaughtered us in an article and knew he had to make amends somehow. Eventually Crossley had to go back and I took Les, who had been in dispute at Luton, until the end of the season. Les had a reputation as a player a little on the wild side but he absolutely flogged himself in training with us, clearly determined to grab any opportunity that arose. He was coming back every afternoon and used to say that every day he spent at Old Trafford was like Christmas Day as far as his career was concerned.

He's not daft and he knew what was expected of him. His confident, almost cocky, approach ensured that he not only enjoyed Wembley – he did a good job. Right from the start he made a good save and handled the ball with the kind of assurance that injects confidence into the whole defence. After he helped us clinch the Cup it was only fair that I should offer him a one-year contract, which he accepted.

The Cup-winning team lined up: Sealey, Ince, Martin, Bruce, Phelan, Pallister, Robson, Webb, McClair, Hughes, Wallace. Subs: Robins, Blackmore.

The Cup put us back into Europe, and I went on holiday that summer thinking, this is the Manchester United I want to be associated with. The season had certainly ended a lot brighter than had been augured after losing two England midfield internationals, Bryan Robson and Neil Webb, for such long periods with serious injuries.

Webb's ruptured Achilles tendon playing for England in Sweden after making just four League appearances for us came as a huge shock. I remember hearing the news away in a hotel and at that point I ordered brandy and went to bed. Neil didn't play for us again until late March, almost the end of the season. Robbo missed three months from the end of December, which left the midfield largely to Paul Ince and Mike Phelan, both new arrivals.

We won only one of our first five League games and it was nip and tuck until the end of the season when we finished in 13th place. The final stages on the way to winning the FA Cup sealed our position in the League because minds had become focused on Wembley. It had been a struggle all season until the Cup sparked us off and saved the day.

I gambled from time to time, for instance playing Neil Webb and Bryan Robson in the semi-final after their long injury problems. As it turned out they both scored and generally turned in solid performances. They tired in the second game but they sensed the importance of the Cup to us at that time and they gave everything. Wembley became our saving grace. It gave us a pot and winning a trophy is important for a club like Manchester United.

My long-term plan is to build a team to last, with people who mirror my approach to the game and can achieve consistency of performance. Winning at Wembley bought me time and I did not feel it was necessary to make any more signings. It was more a question of working towards the development of the players already at Old Trafford. What we needed was a decent respite from injuries and more time to work with our new players.

The big bonus was, of course, to get into Europe again, the arena so beloved by everyone associated with Manchester United – directors, management, players and fans.

SEASON 1989-90
First Division

	P	W	D	L	F	A	PTS
Liverpool	38	23	10	5	78	37	79
Aston Villa	38	21	7	10	57	38	70
Tottenham Hotspur	38	19	6	13	59	47	63
Arsenal	38	18	8	12	54	38	62
Chelsea	38	16	12	10	58	50	60
Everton	38	17	8	13	57	46	59
Southampton	38	15	10	13	71	63	55
Wimbledon	38	13	16	9	57	50	55
Nottingham Forest	38	15	9	14	55	47	54
Norwich City	38	13	14	11	54	52	53
Queens Park Rangers	38	13	11	14	45	44	50
Coventry City	38	14	7	17	39	59	49
MANCHESTER UNITED	38	13	9	16	46	47	48
Manchester City	38	12	12	14	43	52	48
Crystal Palace	38	13	9	16	42	66	48
Derby County	38	13	7	18	43	40	46
Luton Town	38	10	13	15	43	57	43
Sheffield Wednesday	38	11	10	17	35	51	43
Charlton Athletic	38	7	9	22	31	57	30
Millwall	38	5	11	22	39	65	26

APPEARANCES

	League	Littlewoods Cup	FA Cup	Total
Brian McClair	37	3	8	48
Mike Phelan	38	3	7	48
Mark Hughes	36(1)	3	8	47(1)
Gary Pallister	35	3	8	46
Jim Leighton	35	3	7	45
Steve Bruce	34	2	7	43
Lee Martin	28(4)	1	8	37(4)
Paul Ince	25(1)	3	6(1)	34(2)
Danny Wallace	23(3)	2	6(1)	31(4)
Bryan Robson	20	3	4	27
Clayton Blackmore	19(9)	0	2(1)	21(10)
Viv Anderson	14(2)	1	4	19(2)
Mal Donaghy	13(1)	3	1	17(1)
Mike Duxbury	12(7)	1(1)	2(2)	15(10)
Lee Sharpe	13(5)	1(1)	0	14(6)
Neil Webb	10(1)	0	4	14(1)
Mark Robins	10(7)	0	3(3)	13(10)
Russell Beardsmore	8(13)	1	1(2)	10(15)
Colin Gibson	5(1)	0	1(1)	6(2)
Les Sealey	2	0	1	3
Mark Bosnich	1	0	0	1
Giuliano Maiorana	0(1)	0(1)	0	0(2)
Derek Brazil	0(1)	0	0	0(1)
Deiniol Graham	0(1)	0	0	0(1)
Ralph Milne	0(1)	0	0	0(1)

GOALSCORERS

	League	Littlewoods Cup	FA Cup	Total
Mark Hughes	13	0	2	15
Mark Robins	7	0	3	10
Brian McClair	5	0	3	8
Danny Wallace	3	1	2	6
Bryan Robson	2	0	2	4
Clayton Blackmore	2	0	1	3
Steve Bruce	3(inc 1 pen)	0	0	3(inc 1 pen)
Gary Pallister	3	0	0	3
Neil Webb	2	0	1	3
Russell Beardsmore	2	0	0	2
Paul Ince	0	2	0	2
Colin Gibson	1	0	0	1
Lee Martin	0	0	1	1
Mike Phelan	1	0	0	1
Lee Sharpe	1	0	0	1
Own Goals	1	0	0	1
Total	46(inc 1 pen)	3	15	64 (inc 1 pen)

FA CUP

Round 3	Nottingham F	(A)	W	1-0
Round 4	Hereford Utd	(A)	W	1-0
Round 5	Newcastle Utd	(A)	W	3-2
Round 6	Sheffield Utd	(A)	W	1-0
Semi-final	Oldham Athletic		D	3-3 (aet)*
Replay	Oldham Athletic		W	2-1 (aet)
Final	Crystal Palace		D	3-3 (aet)
Replay	Crystal Palace		W	1-0

* at Maine Road

LEAGUE CUP

Round 2/1	Portsmouth	(A)	W	3-2
Round 2/2	Portsmooth	(H)	D	0-0
Round 3	Tottenham	(H)	L	0-3

Chapter Six

VICTORY IN EUROPE

I find it difficult to describe the joy and pride I felt when we triumphed in Europe. Europe has always held a special place in the affections and traditions of everyone associated with Manchester United and to succeed at the first attempt following the five-year ban on English clubs playing in the European competitions was a particular satisfaction. To give United fans their first European trophy for 23 years was also a special delight and an indication, I think, of the progress we are making.

I shall never forget the whole day. The goals were obviously memorable and important, but for me the lasting impression was the atmosphere in the Feyenoord Stadium and watching the jubilation of our supporters in the pouring rain. They enjoyed the occasion and deserved to enjoy it. When you see them as happy as that you know you are with the best club in the world. I am privileged and happy to be with Manchester United, and if ever I have any doubts I have only to think back to that splendid occasion when we beat Barcelona 2-1 in Rotterdam to win the European Cup Winners' Cup.

As we approached the final the first challenge I had to meet was to get the selection and tactics right. I appreciated Johan Cruyff as a good manager after noting some of the things he had done in a match I had watched. I felt I was helped by the fact that word reached me that he had been making inquiries about me so he was obviously wondering about my ability to do things as a tactician. I enjoy a good managerial battle of wits and I tried to read what he would do against us. I worked out that he would play with one centre-back to leave

Ronald Koeman free to set things up. So we put Brian McClair on to Koeman to choke his efforts and make him work hard. It worked perfectly and McClair played a great tactical role in the game. Brian's willingness to run and run stifled Koeman's efforts. It meant of course that we could no longer play Brian wide on the right with Lee Sharpe on the left-wing.

I also knew that Bryan Robson and Paul Ince had to be at the heart of midfield. Ince comes alive on big occasions so it was a straight choice between Mike Phelan and Neil Webb for the third midfield place. Phelan had to be the one because he is quicker than Neil and because his running off the ball was always going to be important. It meant I had to disappoint Neil and it is never easy to do that to players, especially to one of his reputation and standing in the game. I had left him out of the League game at Highbury and he was not happy. He gets a big media explosion every time he is dropped and after my experience with Jim Leighton you have to consider this kind of situation and the effect it might have on the rest of the team. You don't really want to generate the wrong kind of publicity if you can avoid it. Sometimes a controversial decision can become more talked about than the actual game and detract from the build-up and job in hand. It's why these days I sometimes delay announcing my teams until the day of the match. The Press can be perverse and make someone's disappointment seem more important than what it is all about, the match itself.

I told Neil on the morning of the match and he said he had been half-expecting it though that wouldn't of course have made it any less disappointing for him. The back four picked itself. Clayton Blackmore had been marvellous all season at left-back and had scored important goals such as the one in the FA Charity Shield against Liverpool and our first goal back in Europe when he scored against Pecsi Munkas. He had also grabbed a very valuable one against Montpellier in France, and who can forget his cannonball free kick against Arsenal in the Rumbelows?

Denis Irwin had had a very good first season and made a lot of goals with his crosses and corner kicks. Steve Bruce and Gary Pallister picked themselves at centre-back and so with Mark Hughes and Lee Sharpe our main attackers we had a straightforward 4-4-2 formation, the British system which has served our clubs so well over the years, especially in European competition. It has been tried and tested many times.

The big gamble I took was in goal with Les Sealey who had had a bad knee injury in the Rumbelows Cup final against Sheffield Wednesday. Gary Walsh had replaced him and had played in the last League game before the final. He let a softish goal in very early, though that didn't really influence my decision to bring Les back in. I just felt it was better to have an experienced lad in goal for such an important occasion.

Les had not trained up until arriving in Rotterdam so I gave him a rigorous test the day before the match. I wanted to satisfy myself he could handle it OK. In fact, with his bubbly character, Les was bound to come through and wouldn't tire to a degree which would affect his goalkeeping.

As it turned out he did not have a lot to do until late on when we were under some pressure. If the game had gone into extra-time I was actually going to substitute him because his knee had started to swell up and he was limping. We hung on after looking so comfortable early on in a match which I thought notable for its nervousness.

Our first goal came with a nice little chip in by Bryan Robson from a free kick which the goalkeeper decided to come for. I knew he was never going to get there in time and mentally I willed him to keep coming! He did as well and he got himself into no man's-land. Steve Bruce rushed in and was there first for an excellent header which was going in when, to make sure, Mark Hughes helped it on its way and so claimed the goal.

I thought we were playing quite well and we increased the pace in a first half which I thought was fairly low-key. After the interval Barcelona produced far more energy and determination. There was more purpose to their game, though I must confess that once in front I felt fairly comfortable about us winning. The United team have a habit of getting to your nerve ends but they eased the uncertainty when they scored a tremendous second goal. Brian Moore on television said Mark Hughes had lost his chance when he took the ball wide, but he produced a stunning finish to give us a two-goal lead. He had both feet off the ground when he shot. Other players were screaming for a pass but Mark is a born striker and he was having none of it. He took the responsibility on board and his goal reflected a player in really confident mood.

I think Mark went into that final against Barcelona with something to prove. He had had a rotten time with them and had been shipped out on loan to Bayern Munich and I was pleased he was able to have the last word on this occasion. It was a goal worthy of winning a European final. Barcelona appealed for offside but their defence stepped forward too late as television showed.

Anyway, once that second goal had gone in with just 14 minutes to go, I thought it was all over. Barcelona had other ideas and just four minutes later Ronald Koeman scored from a free-kick, one of his specialities. A lot of people thought Les might have done better with it, but by that time he was starting to struggle with his knee.

The last ten-minute period was a real nail-biter. Barcelona had a goal chalked off but it was well offside. The biggest heart-stopping moment came when Clayton Blackmore kicked off the line. There were only three minutes to go and everyone who saw it will remember Clayton for ever. Les had come out and Gary Pallister went with their man to the byeline. The ball came across to Laudrup and he side-footed it towards the empty net. Clayton had read it brilliantly and the incident was our big bonus. At that point my mind became a blur and I hardly remember the finish.

The closing stages were anxious, but I made us the better team. We handled the whole business comfortably from the build-up to the actual match. Cruyff didn't seem to give us much credit afterwards. He seems to be a manager who has to look for an excuse, but in my book we won it fair and square. It was a great occasion with a reception to match on our return home.

The fans who had been at the game gathered at the airport in Holland to give us a rousing send-off, which I suppose was an indication of what to expect back in Manchester. I think the people at home saw our European success as a tribute to the city and they reacted accordingly. The motorcade went from Manchester Airport into the city centre. The streets were lined with people but when we reached Deansgate they thinned out. When we hit the bridge near the Ramada Hotel, though, it was unbelievable; and when we went into

Salford we were in the heartland of our support historically. We had been on the bus for nearly three hours by then, but suddenly the tiredness lifted as we faced this fantastic support and were reminded that Manchester United are the biggest club in the business.

I had experienced something similar in Aberdeen after we won the same trophy, when the whole town stopped and people came in from the outlying districts. They reckoned there were 500,000 people in the town, more than double the normal population. But the volume of people in Manchester took my breath away, particularly when I saw Manchester City supporters joining in the welcome home! There is tremendous, even bitter, rivalry between us and City, but on this occasion it seemed as if the lads with the blue scarves simply wanted to say 'well done'. A lot of City supporters were on our side for that night at least, which was good to see.

In addition to the tactics, I knew that we had to get our preparation right as well. I am happy to say that we picked an excellent hotel just outside Rotterdam. Everything we asked for was done. We had a conference room for meetings and a games room which included everything imaginable for the players. The after-match buffet was marvellous and in keeping with the way they had looked after us right from day one. Another thing in the build-up which worked well for us was the decision to take Jimmy Steele as masseur. He is one of the great characters of football and has been with Glasgow Celtic for ages. He is a man of 76 now and in his day worked as a second for boxer Freddie Mills. He was with Manchester United for their FA Cup final of 1976 and again the following year when they won it. He is the best masseur in the business and having him there left Jim McGregor free to concentrate on the treatment side of things. At the end we gave him a present of a watch because he won't take a penny for his work – Celtic don't pay him anything for instance – and he was delighted.

He always fights in your corner and is a fiercely protective man. I remember being with Jock Stein and Scotland in Iceland when there was a bad tackle – by Graeme Souness actually – and the Icelandic President had a bit of a go afterwards. Jimmy, going on 70 at the time, actually wanted to fight him, and he was ready again in Rotterdam when one of the television people was shoving a camera almost up my nose.

He revealed another side of his usefulness when the kick-off was delayed for five minutes or so and the players were kept in the dressing-room. I could see the tension mounting but Jimmy immediately responded by starting to sing and banter. It took the edge off them and they were able to go out in good shape.

Even though I say it myself, our whole operation was planned to perfection. Even the training ground we borrowed from a local amateur club was exactly what we needed and we used to have anything up to a thousand people watching us. After the first session we happened to mention that the grass was a bit long, and sure enough the next day it had been cut. Everything simply fell into place, starting in fact from the outset of the competition.

For we could not have asked for a more accommodating tie to mark our return to European football and our first game following the five-year exile. To put it bluntly Pecsi Munkas was a nice easy one for starters. I went to see them play and they were a tidy side but not one to scare us. We still managed to look nervous, though, when we played the first leg until Clayton Blackmore and Neil Webb gave us a 2-0 win. I perhaps erred on the cautious side for the return in Hungary and played my most experienced people, including Viv Anderson for what was one of his last appearances for the club. Brian McClair gave us a close 1-0 win, but it was in fact more comfortable than the score suggested.

We got an even better break for the next round when we were drawn against Wrexham. It was virtually next-door with no travelling involved, and there were never any real problems about winning 3-0 at home and then 2-0 away. One of the most satisfying aspects was that winning put us through to the quarter-finals, which was a nice feeling because the competition went on ice until the following March and it meant we had something built in for the end of the season, regardless of progress on other fronts.

When March finally came round the only thing that really worried me was the state of our pitch. It had been causing me concern for some time because it had deteriorated and our game relies heavily on accurate passing and good control. The first leg was at home and it was important to produce our football because after watching Montpellier I expected a difficult time. In fact we opened well and made the perfect start with a great goal of quality from Brian McClair involving a perfect finish. However, when our team hit a peak they so often seem to tumble off it and we allowed the French team back into the game to equalise. Their boy struck a long-range shot as if to say, 'I'll just have a bang with it', and Lee Martin put it in his own goal. Les Sealey looked stunned as it flew in, almost too stunned to be angry. Actually it set his whole game off and there was no way he was gong to be beaten again that night, though that did not alter the fact that a 1-1 result was hardly the best score to take to a place like Montpellier for the second leg.

They had the advantage of an away goal to count double in the event of a goalless draw. But ironically the knowledge that we had to score resulted in us thinking in very positive terms. We knew it would be a very tight game and that only our best shot would suffice. At least we had our strongest team out and I was delighted with the attitude of the players. I have got to add that we also had some luck going for us. They had a few bits and pieces, but Clayton Blackmore hit a smashing free kick which swerved in and I could see them deflate. I was confident our stamina would see us finish strongly and when Steve Bruce converted a penalty we were heading for victory and the tie went to us 2-0.

It was a really top performance. We kept possession and were masters on the night despite the fact that many of the pundits, and perhaps even some of our followers, had written us off. Our travelling support was wonderful and created a European night to savour.

Excitement gathered for the semi-finals and that's when we got our next break with Juventus drawn against Barcelona to leave us with Legia Warsaw. We got the plum among the last four and maybe that was the moment when our name came to be written on the Cup. The Poles had beaten Sampdoria so they could hardly be disregarded, but we had certainly got the one I wanted to leave two of the most experienced and accomplished clubs in the world facing each other.

We put on one hell of a performance in the first leg in Poland to win 3-1. They scored first but Brian McClair took only a minute to equalise. We went on in the second half to score through Mark Hughes and Steve Bruce, helped by the fact that they had Marek Jozwiak sent off for pulling down Lee Sharpe.

Lee was really on fire against the Poles and he was the scorer when we drew the second leg 1-1 at Old Trafford. We were a bit muted that night because the game came just three days after losing the Rumbelows Cup final and we were in a rather depressed mood. We knew we were sitting on a two-goal lead from the first leg and indeed that was when we won the tie.

Steve Bruce's goal in that first leg was his seventh in six games, and only two had been from the penalty spot. He could do nothing wrong at that period and in fact went on to complete a splendid scoring season with a total of 19 goals, 11 of them penalties but eight from open play which is a more than useful contribution from a centre-half. Steve has always been a mixture of ability and enthusiasm, and he was full of himself around that time. All he could talk about was scoring goals and declaring that he wanted to play centre-forward. He used to go on about wasting his time in defence and that McClair should swap places with him. McClair would rise to the bait and explain that Bruce was just a Geordie deserving of everyone's sympathy. Mark Hughes would just smile. When you carry the responsibility for scoring it's another matter!

We were hot in the closing stages of the season, except for a couple of League defeats just before the Cup Winners' Cup final, which I think can be put down to thoughts drifting towards Rotterdam in anticipation of Barcelona. Certainly around the European semi-finals we were really buzzing which made our performance in the final of the Rumbelows so much more disappointing. We were favourites but it didn't show in the result.

In fairness we should have murdered Sheffield Wednesday in football terms. We were all over them and they spent most of the time simply defending. Good luck to them, they won the Cup and it's their name in the record books. But let's get it right. I read some of the critics afterwards saying that Wednesday were the better team. That's nonsense – they were never in the game. That was simply the Press pandering to Ron Atkinson because they liked the line of a former Manchester United manager beating his successor.

Things fell into place for Ron with his association with the media and the papers liked the twist of him returning to win against his old club. At the end of the day I accept that we had only ourselves to blame

91

because I think we made the fatal mistake of under-estimating them. We had just had the impressive victory over Legia at Old Trafford and we had the return just three days after playing at Wembley to think about. If it hadn't been for that second leg I believe we would have started at a higher pace.

I was on to the players before the game but the message just didn't sink in. I left Mike Phelan and Mal Donaghy on the bench and played a midfield of Bryan Robson, Paul Ince and Neil Webb, a tried and trusted combination and the first time incidentally that that particular trio had played together in a losing team. We debated before the match whether to leave Webb out and play Phelan instead with McClair more central in a 4-4-2 formation, and if we had done so I think we would have won the match. Still, it is always easy with hindsight. The bigger problem was our soft approach which resulted in us not keeping possession long enough. We were chasing them at times instead of controlling the game. There was an attitude in the team of, 'Let's just give it to "Sharpey" and he will win it for us'. He was in hot form but although he is a good player one man doesn't win on his own at Wembley . The game in fact went over his head. They scored just before half-time and when that happens in a cup final you know you have a big job on your hands.

There was another factor as well behind the scenes and a most disturbing one because it was at this time that I lost my right-hand man in Archie Knox. I didn't actually know it at Wembley but looking back, there was a funny atmosphere. Once I have done my bit with a team talk before a game I move away from the players and let them get on with their own individual preparation. Archie would take over as coach, and he kept things going. The other staff said afterwards that it wasn't the same as usual. Archie was subdued and again, looking back, I think it was at this point that he had decided to join Glasgow Rangers.

When a guy leaves a job there is always a chain reaction, so when Graeme Souness left Ibrox to take over at Liverpool there was a vacancy. It was fairly obvious that Walter Smith, a good friend of mine – so much so that I took him as my assistant when I had my spell as manager of Scotland – would step up to become the new manager. One or two names were mentioned for the assistant's job, but I never thought for one minute that Walter would come for Archie. I never dreamt either that Archie would even think about leaving.

Somewhere along the line though, Walter had decided that Archie was the man he wanted. I suppose, again easier with hindsight, that it figured because the two of them had grown up together and had become firm friends when they were together at Dundee United. I remembered later that Archie had asked me earlier in the month if he could go up to Scotland for a little break, and naturally I told him to go right ahead and enjoy a few days with his wife Janice. He actually stayed with Walter Smith and that must have been when all the seeds were sown.

The hypocrisy of it all was that while Rangers were complaining and haggling over the approach for Souness they were doing exactly the same thing with Archie. Their Chairman, David Murray, had adopted quite a moral stance and Rangers were screaming blue murder but were at it all the time themselves behind the backs of Manchester United. The bottom line in this kind of situation is that at the end of the day there is absolutely nothing you can do about it!

Ironically, I had kept two tickets for the Rumbelows Cup final for Walter and on the day I got a fax to say he was not coming. I know why now! The following day he phoned me back at the ground to say he had a tough one for me and he went on to explain that he had offered Archie the job as his assistant. I told him I thought he was a friend of mine as well, but he explained that he needed the best man he could get which was Archie, and I could hardly fault his thinking on that one. All the same I said that if we were going official then the answer was no he couldn't have him because he was under contract.

I had Archie in and his explanation was simply: 'It's the money'. I replied: 'Archie, the football is crap up there and you know it.' It's true, too. The standard has always been high in England, and it is more so now because in my view Scottish football has gone backwards in the last year or so. At this point I explained that I would have to speak to the Chairman in the hope of offering him better personal terms to stay. I also said I was extremely disappointed. Remember this was all happening just two days before a European semi-final, not the ideal time to lose your coach and the man arguably the closest to the players.

Anyway we came back and made him a terrific offer and he was already the highest paid assistant in the game. It was all so terribly upsetting because it was undoing the foundations I had taken a long time to build. The staff was all in place and it was a good one with everyone working harmoniously together.

I take absolutely nothing away from Archie's contribution. He had worked himself into the ground for us. He was always a beast for work and he had been important not only at first team level but in what he had done to create our school of excellence and get the schoolboy operation set up with Brian Kidd.

I had known him for a long time and it was a partnership of trust and respect. I said to him: 'You have done so much and now you want to throw it all away by leaving on the eve of United's first success in Europe for 23 years.'

His move could not even be delayed until the end of the season. Murray demanded an instant appointment and it was all part of the big money deal they were dangling in front of him. He was very low after the Legia game and I could see he was having a big struggle inside him. I still didn't think he would go. I thought commonsense would prevail, but it became obvious as time went by that he had made up his mind. The money involved was important to him, and one of the things you can never argue against when it comes to this kind of situation is the cash.

If a person is motivated by money or thinks the security involved is important to him there is not a lot you can do. If it is a matter of ambition, quality of work or the environment of the job then you can argue a case. But this was financial, and I came to realise that I was battering my head against a brick wall with him. He had made up his mind to leave Old Trafford and that was that. I would have thought that he would have appreciated that we had done most of the hard work and that we could look forward to reaping the benefit.

Manchester United represent the biggest challenge in football and will remain so at least until that elusive League Championship returns to Old Trafford after all these years. Archie, I'm afraid, has opted for an easier life. Management of United is the most difficult job of the lot. You need character and tremendous endurance to pursue it and I wonder at times how long I will be able to last out.

I'm 50, which I don't consider really old, and hopefully I can go on for another five or six years, but you certainly require colossal energy to stay on top of it. But Archie is younger than me and I would have thought that the challenge at this stage of his career would have been too compelling for him to walk away from.

Rangers, with their resources, are going to win the Scottish League for the next ten years at least and that to me doesn't involve the kind of test I am looking for. It certainly does not represent the challenge implicit at Old Trafford. I played for Rangers and they are a terrific club. I know you can argue that every job is a challenge but the Rangers job is not one for me. It doesn't contain what is important in life, but Archie did not see it that way. Rangers pale into insignificance when compared with what Manchester United is about.

I always remember Graeme Souness saying after becoming manager at Ibrox that Rangers are the second biggest club after Manchester United. Then significantly, after coming down to take charge of Liverpool, he changed tack slightly and said that Liverpool are the most successful club in Britain for the last 25 years, a subtle but important distinction!

The two Chairmen agreed appropriate compensation and Archie's departure was settled. But the money we received did not compensate for being without him at such an important stage of the season, with Europe coming to a climax and with all the stress and decisions involved.

The rest of the staff at Old Trafford could not understand him. They see people striving all their lives to be in the kind of position we had arrived at, and here was a man turning his back on it. The sad part was that Archie had earned the glory of it through sheer hard work and effort. So when it was all agreed I asked him when they expected him to start at Ibrox and he replied: 'Tomorrow.' There was nothing more to say. I thanked him for what he had done for me and wished him all the best. There was no point in parting enemies. I respected the work he had done at Old Trafford and while I did not agree with his decision I had to respect the offer he had received. We have spoken only once since, and that was after winning the European Cup Winners' Cup.

I suppose Archie lives for the minute and he has moved into a different world. He is a hard worker and a decent lad, though it wasn't the first time he had left me. In 1983 though, it was right for him. He had been manager at Forfar before joining me at Aberdeen and he wanted to have a go as manager of a club on his own again. So when he got a chance to go to Dundee I said: 'Off you go'. It was right for him at that stage of his career. He did a decent job there, a much bigger club than Forfar of course. I replaced him that time with a young lad, which didn't quite work out.

I asked him if he would like to come back to Pittodrie when we were at the World Cup in Mexico in 1986 and he immediately accepted. Then when I moved to Manchester I took him with me. It had all fallen neatly into place for him. It was a good association. We had arguments of course, but that's one of the reasons you have an assistant – in order to assess the pros and cons of problems. He certainly always gave me total commitment.

All good things come to an end some time I suppose and it was just another problem. You get plenty of those at Manchester United. There is always a dilemma around the corner. I have never enjoyed a period of tranquility. You don't even get two days without having to sort something or other out. It's the immensity of the place. Archie went and we had to get on with the job without him. The immediate requirement was to get our semi-final opponents watched and at the same time keep track of the other semi with a view to playing the winners in the final.

Les Kershaw went to watch Barcelona in Saragossa while Brian Kidd scouted out Juventus, much the same as I had done with Aberdeen when we were heading for our final against Real Madrid.

Brian Kidd went on to play an increasingly important role. He had, of course, played through the ranks at Old Trafford after joining as a local schoolboy star from Collyhurst where he went to the same school as Nobby Stiles. His career took him to a number of clubs, including a spell with Manchester City, but I think United were his first and last love. He had become associated with the club again in the area of football in the community and then I had pulled him in to share in our expansion of youth development. He did an excellent job with schoolboy coaching and eventually I took him on to the permanent staff to do even more in the field of finding and signing

*Heading for my first trophy with Manchester United as I lead the team out
at Wembley for the FA Cup final of 1990*

*Left: They can paint the crossbar without a ladder: Peter Schmeichel and Gary Pallister.
Right: Dion Dublin, the £1 million signing from Cambridge United*

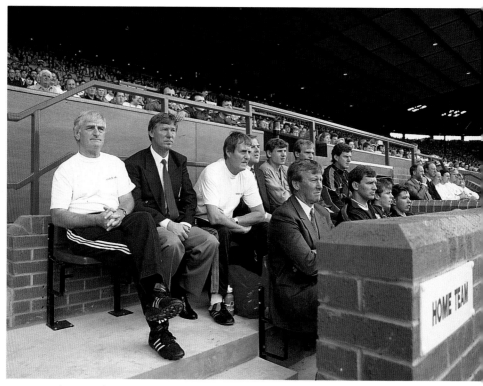

The new dug-out at Old Trafford with physiotherapist Jim McGregor on my right and kitman Norman Davies on my left

The back-room boys: Norman Davies, Archie Knox, myself and Jim McGregor

Lee Martin's moment of glory as he scores to win the FA Cup in the replay against Crystal Palace in 1990

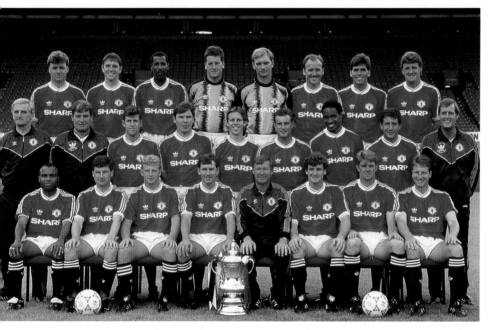

The proud FA Cup winners of 1990

Support for Manchester United is fantastic and the demand for autographs endless

Barclays bubbly for Manager of the Month

Mark Hughes scoring a typically spectacular goal to clinch the European Cup Winners' Cup

Lining up for the 1991 crunch against Barcelona in the Feyenoord Stadium

*Gary Pallister parades the FA Charity Shield at Wembley after sharing in a
1-1 draw with Liverpool*

Mike Phelan with the Rumbelows Cup after playing a key role in the victory against Nottingham Forest at Wembley

Bridging the gap in Europe ... myself with the European Cup Winners' Cup and Sir Matt Busby with a replica of the European Cup he won for Manchester United in 1968

The victory parade back home in Manchester after beating Barcelona – and what a fantastic welcome

youngsters. It didn't do us any harm at all to have a former playing hero now actively involved in talking to the mothers and fathers of youngsters who interested us. It was nice to add another United old boy to the staff.

More recently, I promoted him to first team coach after considering a number of other possibilities. His enthusiasm and coaching abillty have once again come through and I am very happy to have him as the successor to Archie Knox.

I believe I have built a good training staff, with Bryan 'Pop' Robson, the former Newcastle and West Ham forward, joining us after running the school of excellence we set up in the North East. Jimmy Ryan, another former player from the Sixties was also brought back to help with the reserves following the departure of Brian Whitehouse and his eventual return to link up with Ron Atkinson at Aston Villa. Jimmy played at Luton and managed them after enjoying a long successful spell in the United States, so he brings a wide range of experience with him.

I suppose our season in the League was again haunted by inconsistency, though this was undoubtedly influenced in the later stages by two cup finals, with all the injuries and extra pressures those involved.

We made a good start with a 2-0 win at home to Coventry, and a goalless draw at Leeds three days later wasn't bad. We lost at Sunderland but came back with a couple of wins before losing at Liverpool in a run which was to reflect our lack of consistency. Then the start of our European campaign took our minds off the bread and butter stuff, for though we won the match immediately after Pecsi Munkas, we promptly lost two on the trot, along with sharing the spoils at Maine Road in a 3-3 draw.

At least we had got Lee Sharpe back in action following his recovery from a hernia operation in the close season. He had in fact played very little the previous season and I was keen to see him playing again. However, his first game back was not exactly an auspicious occasion for it was the day we lost 1-0 at home to Arsenal in a game which hit the headlines for all the wrong reasons. Some called it a brawl; I thought it was more handbags at dawn. Nevertheless, it had serious consequences for both clubs and was not at all welcome

97

following the tunnel incident with John Fashanu and Viv Anderson the previous season.

Anders Limpar, the Swedish international winger, had been needling away and getting up the noses of a number of our players. I have got to say that he is that type of player. Feeling crept in from both sides with Brian McClair, unusually for him, exchanging words with Nigel Winterburn, the Gunners' full-back. The explosion came when Limpar went into a tackle on Denis Irwin which could easily have seriously hurt him. It carried on from there and for a brief couple of minutes everyone piled in, though I don't think there were any serious blows struck. Certainly no-one packed a Fashanu-type punch.

Ironically George Graham and I get on very well. We are fellow Scots in English football with a great deal of mutual respect. So it was all a bit embarrassing when it hit the newspapers in a big way, and in my opinion was greatly overplayed. The FA held an inquiry and both clubs suffered the most dire punishment possible. Arsenal had two points deducted while we had one struck off. As always, the media loved it and made a meal of it. I went to the disciplinary hearing and there was no-one of real substance on it. In fact I got the distinct impression that there were one or two who didn't care for Manchester United. The meeting was a shambles and it's my opinion that the decisions had been taken long before the meeting started.

What I find difficult to understand is why we were taken to court and punished so severely when others have escaped disciplinary action for what have been far worse incidents. Birmingham, for instance, once had a thousand spectators on the pitch and the referee was attacked but I don't recall anything being done by way of disciplinary action.

I recall a dust-up at a Crystal Palace and Wimbledon match which the FA chose to ignore. Sunderland and Wimbledon had 16 players involved in a flare-up, but again it was never the subject of any inquiry.

So why were Manchester United and Arsenal picked on to be made examples of?

I believe it is because we are high-profile clubs who sell newspapers and the Press demanded a *cause célèbre*. The result was that the FA moved the goalposts to suit the media and pander to them.

They perhaps also felt that if the papers weren't handed United and Arsenal on a punishment plate they would swing the spotlight on to the authorities and give them a blast about behaviour.

I was delighted Arsenal still won the League, despite the two-point deduction. That was justice, but I was still left with a very real concern for the way justice is dispensed generally in football by the FA.

I was also greatly bothered by the internal action taken by both clubs. I felt it was quite wrong of the Arsenal board to fine their manager. George Graham had not been involved personally, and I consider it an insult to a manager of his standing to hand out a punishment as if he needed to be reminded of the importance of standards of behaviour. I felt it demeaning and still consider it was unnecessary.

Of course, a manager is the man responsible for discipline at his club, which is precisely the reason why he should have been given support as opposed to being put in the dock along with the real offenders. Arsenal set a dangerous precedent which one day could backfire on them.

Perhaps the Arsenal board panicked, and they regret their action. I hope so. I might add that with hindsight I felt I also acted unwisely with my own internal disciplinary action.

I fined three players – Brian McClair, Paul Ince and Denis Irwin. Two of them are rarely booked and can hardly be described as problem players, while Paul Ince may do a lot of yapping which upsets referees, but he is not a violent man. I felt embarrassed fining them because they conduct themselves with great dignity. I did it because I felt the club and myself were under pressure and people were expecting some positive action.

I regret it now though, and with a better perspective I should simply have talked to them. They knew they were wrong to react to provocation and the fine served no purpose except perhaps to make the FA feel good and give the Press more ammunition.

Strangely, after the Arsenal game we launched into a great spell, losing only once in a 24-match run to capture the kind of consistency I had been looking for. We turned in a particulariy devastating performance at Arsenal as we turned our attention to the Rumbelows Cup. We won 6-2 with the help of a hat-trick from Lee Sharpe. To score six at Highbury was special, but the main significance was that it signalled the arrival of a special talent in the form of Sharpe after he had battled back from his injury problems. He revealed an exciting pace in a team I picked specifically to play Arsenal after losing to them at Old Trafford in the fateful League game.

I decided to leave Webb out and play Danny Wallace through the middle with Hughes, leaving Sharpe to play a little deeper then usual. They found him difficult to pick up. They didn't expect it and it became one of those magic nights. Wallace was brilliant at drifting into space. Indeed, for a spell around that stage of the season he was the player I had envisaged when I bought him from Southampton.

Arsenal actually got back to 3-2 at one point but we hit them with three more goals in a match handled incredibly well by both teams, considering the fracas of the League game just a month before. We then switched Cups to get through the third round of the FA competition at home to QPR before travelling to Southampton for the quarter-final in the Rumbelows. Hughes scored to get us a 1-1 draw. He had been in brilliant scoring form for a few weeks and he nabbed a hat-trick in the replay at Old Trafford for a 3-2 victory.

We could really have done without that replay because the games were coming at us thick and fast on three Cup fronts. Three days later we got through 1-0 in the FA Cup at home to Bolton with Hughes again the scorer.

This brought us to two tough ties in the Rumbelows against Leeds United. For some reason there was a lot of bad feeling in those games and I think it stemmed from aggression on the terraces. The rivalry between Manchester United and Leeds has been fraught with problems in recent seasons, and I hope that the fact that they have just pipped us for the Championship will not add to an already difficult enough situation. In the first game at Old Trafford there were three players booked and a few face-to-face confrontations. I think Howard Wilkinson thought Leeds were going to win, but I kept looking at Mel Sterland facing Lee Sharpe and I concluded that Lee was too much on song for him. Sharpe scored in a 2-1 win along with McClair and I think we deserved to be ahead.

Nevertheless, there was a little anxiety going to Elland Road for the second leg with only a one-goal advantage. Sharpe scored again, though, to give us a double win. There were a lot of bad things in the second game which is really best forgotten. There were lessons for both clubs from the encounter. Ironically, I get on well with Howard Wilkinson and there is a similar respect and friendship between the two staffs, but there is a lot of aggression in the Leeds game and they have the most intimidating support in football.

Sandwiched between the two Rumbelows ties was the fifth round of the FA Cup at Norwich. We lost 2-1 but nobody seemed too bothered as we headed for the quarter-final against Montpellier in the European competition, with a Rumbelows place at Wembley already booked. I was not very happy, though, because we had been asked to travel all the way to Carrow Road for a Monday night match to fit in with satellite television.

The problem has surfaced again following the agreement with the BBC and BSkyB. The satellite people like to have live football on a Monday evening, and if you are putting a massive £304 million into the pot you are entitled to be the piper calling the tune. But in my view Monday night football on a regular basis has to be resisted. Our Norwich Cup-tie was a classic example of what is wrong with the idea. How can you ask supporters to travel all that distance on a Monday? If the match had been played as originally scheduled on a Saturday people at least have a chance of being able to make it without have to get time off work.

One accepts midweek replays as unavoidable, but to kick off an FA Cup-tie on a Monday is wrong in my view. If satellite television has its way, Monday night football could become a regular feature of our sporting calendar, bringing in its wake a lot of other problems like being asked to play 48 hours before, say, an important European tie.

It must be opposed. I hasten to add that I am not blaming the TV switch for our defeat at Norwich. Losing was more to do with the game being sandwiched between the two semi-final ties with Leeds. The frequency of playing was beginning to catch up with us.

It also hit us in the League, I think. Right in the middle of a run of five Cup-ties we played Liverpool at Old Trafford in a televised match. Steve Bruce hit a penalty to give us a 1-1 draw, but we really needed to win, and had we done so we would have moved into third place in the League.

101

We were also caught in a backlash following the testing ties against Leeds and all the other games we played at that point in the season. We lost three title games on the trot, against Sheffield United, Everton and Chelsea. We halted the nosedive with a couple of draws and then won a few, but the die was cast. It was going to be a Cup season and we finished sixth in the League. I am sure it would have been much higher if we had not been involved in two Cup finals.

I am certainly not complaining because It was a magic end to the season with that fabulous, unforgettable night in Rotterdam to win the European Cup Winners' Cup.

The team which beat Barcelona lined up: Sealey, Irwin, Blackmore, Bruce, Phelan, Pallister, Robson, Ince, McClair, Hughes, Sharp. Subs: Webb, Donaghy, Robins, Wallace, Walsh.

When people have spent fortunes following your team and you have been able to give them something special as we did that night then it becomes one of the great days of your life. It registers as one of the landmarks which will endure for everyone there. Supporters will recall the occasion fondly and when the players meet up in later life it will be a source of rich satisfaction. They will regard it as a significant piece of their life.

We received a great Press and were on the front pages for all the right reasons. I'll certainly never forget Clayton Blackmore's late saver or the gamble with Les Sealey. His antics at Wembley when he had refused to come off after cutting his knee wide open set the seal on the determination to succeed we saw in Rotterdam. Les had come near to hitting Jim McGregor when our physiotherapist wanted to have him off. I think Jim was close to belting Les, too, because it was a bad one and by rights it should have been treated in the dressing-room. He did in fact faint at the airport on the way home from the Rumbelows final and his next game was the European final three weeks later. The risk proved worth it and it all added up to a satisfying season.

Apart from the obvious achievement of appearing in two finals I was quietly pleased with the unbeaten run of 24 games with only one defeat. There was more than a hint of the stability I was striving for. I could see a pattern as things began to fall into place and generally I had a better control of the situation.

102

SEASON 1990-91
First Division

	P	W	D	L	F	A	PTS
Arsenal	38	24	13	1	74	18	83
Liverpool	38	23	7	8	77	40	76
Crystal Palace	38	20	9	9	50	41	69
Leeds United	38	19	7	12	65	47	64
Manchester City	38	17	11	10	64	53	62
MANCHESTER UNITED	38	16	12	10	58	45	59
Wimbledon	38	14	14	10	53	46	56
Nottingham Forest	38	14	12	12	65	50	54
Everton	38	13	12	13	50	46	51
Tottenham Hotspur	38	11	16	11	51	50	49
Chelsea	38	13	10	15	58	69	49
Queens Park Rangers	38	12	10	16	44	53	46
Sheffield United	38	13	7	18	36	55	46
Southampton	38	12	9	17	58	69	45
Norwich City	38	13	6	19	41	64	45
Coventry City	38	11	11	16	42	49	44
Aston Villa	38	9	14	15	46	58	41
Luton Town	38	10	7	21	42	61	37
Sunderland	38	8	10	20	38	60	34
Derby County	38	5	9	24	37	75	24

APPEARANCES

	League	Rumbelows Cup	ECWC	FA Cup	Total
Gary Pallister	36	9	9	3	57
Clayton Blackmore	35	9	9	3	56
Brian McClair	34(2)	9	9	3	55(2)
Les Sealey	31	8	8	3	50
Denis Irwin	33(1)	7(1)	6	3	49(2)
Steve Bruce	31	7	8	3	49
Mark Hughes	29(2)	9	7(1)	3	48(3)
Mike Phelan	30(3)	7(1)	8	1	46(4)
Neil Webb	31(1)	7	6	2	46(1)
Paul Ince	31	6	7	2	46
Lee Sharpe	20(3)	7	6(2)	3	36(5)
Bryan Robson	15(2)	5	4	3	27(2)
Mal Donaghy	17(8)	3(4)	2(3)	0	22(15)
Danny Wallace	13(6)	1(3)	2(1)	0(1)	16(11)
Lee Martin	7(7)	2(2)	3(2)	1	13(11)
Mark Robins	7(12)	0(3)	2(1)	0(1)	9(17)
Russell Beardsmore	5(7)	1	1(1)	0	7(8)
Gary Walsh	5	0	1	0	6
Viv Anderson	1	1	1	0	3
Darren Ferguson	2(3)	0	0	0	2(3)
Mark Bosnich	2	0	0	0	2
Ryan Giggs	1(1)	0	0	0	1(1)
Andrei Kanchelskis	1	0	0	0	1
Jim Leighton	0	1	0	0	1
Neil Whitworth	1	0	0	0	1
Paul Wratten	0(2)	0	0	0	0(2)

GOALSCORERS

	League	Rumbelows Cup	ECWC	FA Cup	Total
Mark Hughes	10	6	3	2	21
Brian McClair	13	2	4	2	21
Steve Bruce	13(7)	2(2)	4(2)	0	19(11)
Lee Sharpe	2	6	1	0	9
Clayton Blackmore	4(1)	2	2	0	8(1)
Mark Robins	4	0	1	0	5
Neil Webb	3	1	1	0	5
Danny Wallace	3	1	0	0	4
Paul Ince	3	0	0	0	3
Viv Anderson	0	1	0	0	1
Ryan Giggs	1	0	0	0	1
Gary Pallister	0	0	1	0	1
Mike Phelan	1	0	0	0	1
Bryan Robson	1	0	0	0	1
Total	58(8)	21(2)	17(2)	4	100 (12)

* bracketed figures denote penalties

EUROPEAN CUP WINNERS' CUP

Round 1/1	Pecsi Munkas	(H)	W	2-0
Round 1/2	Pecsi Munkas	(A)	W	1-0
Round 2/1	Wrexham	(H)	W	3-0
Round 2/2	Wrexham	(A)	W	2-0
Round 3/1	Montpellier	(H)	D	1-1
Round 3/2	Montpellier	(A)	W	2-0
Semi-final/1	Legia Warsaw	(A)	W	3-1
Semi-final/2	Legia Warsaw	(H)	D	1-1
Final	Barcelona		W	2-1*

* at Rotterdam

FA CUP

Round 3	QPR	(H)	W	2-1
Round 4	Bolton W	(H)	W	1-0
Round 5	Norwich	(A)	L	1-2

LEAGUE CUP

Round 2/1	Halifax T	(A)	W	3-1
Round 2/2	Halifax T	(H)	W	2-1
Round 3	Liverpool	(H)	W	3-1
Round 4	Arsenal	(A)	W	6-2
Round 5	Southampton	(A)	D	1-1
Replay	Southampton	(H)	W	3-2
Semi-final/1	Leeds United	(H)	W	2-1
Semi-final/2	Leeds United	(A)	W	1-0
Final	Sheffield Wednesday	Wembley	L	0-1

Chapter Seven

SO NEAR

Flushed with the success of Europe, I stuck my neck right out. Some no doubt considered I was foolish to be so bold but I honestly thought we were ripe for a serious assault on the League Championship. It was not a matter of getting carried away but simply a declaration of intent for the supporters of Manchester United.

When you beat a club like Barcelona and you know you have a young side thirsting for more, you have a right to be ambitious and let your feelings be known. It's at a time like that when your followers want to hear you thinking aloud. You cannot 'ca canny', as we say in Scotland, all the time. You cannot always shelter the players from the demands and expectations of the fans. At some stage you have to stand up and be counted.

We know now of course the cruel end to the season and how our dreams faded away on the last lap but that is how I felt the morning after our European victory. 'Let's go for it,' I thought.

I felt I had control of the situation and I could see a pattern emerging not only in the way the first team were operating but in the structure of the whole club. Things were coming together nicely but at the same time I knew that I had to improve certain areas if we were to capture the consistency which is the hallmark of teams which win the English League. I wanted a wide right player and filling this gap became my next task in the transfer market. I was attracted by reports of Andrei Kanchelskis a Ukrainian winger and international with the then Soviet Union. He was quick and had a sturdy build for a boy of

21. Also at a fee of £650,000 he was not expensive by present day standards. We had him watched and I went to see him play for the Soviets against Germany. The Chairman and I then completed the deal through a chain of agents and interpreters. All things considered, I saw him as a great investment. We had been alerted first by a Norwegian journalist who had sent me videos of him playing. The transfer had taken a few weeks and he had in fact made his debut and played one game near the end of the previous season but there was a hitch with his work permit and he wasn't really with us until the following season. I know he will become a really important player for us and I was pleased to see him enjoying a good run with the CIS in the European Championships in Sweden last summer.

The goalkeeping situation was not clear. I had been forced to accept that Jim Leighton's career at Old Trafford was over despite the fact that I knew he was still a good goalkeeper. Les Sealey had done brilliantly for us but his contract was up and he was insisting he would only sign on again for us if I gave him an agreement for two years. We had to differ because I didn't feel he was the long term answer for us and I would only offer him a one-year deal. I thought Gary Walsh would soon be back to take care of the future and in the meantime I had been impressed by reports we had been given about Peter Schmeichel, the Danish international, from Brondby. I knew all about him because I had tried for him a couple of seasons before. At that stage he was in contract and the fee was ridiculously high. Now, though, he was out of his agreement and I discovered that he was interested in joining Manchester United.

I asked Alan Hodgkinson, our goalkeeping coach, to watch him over six games at international and club level. Alan's report was quite to the point, saying clearly he considered him the best goalkeeper in Europe. He reckoned that the king-sized Peter would be an absolute star in our team because he had everything needed, ranging through physique, courage and ability.

With our minds made up, we managed to buy him for £505,000 which was tremendous business for us. Everything that has happened since with Peter has borne out our highest hopes and I was delighted to see him playing for Denmark in the final of the European Championships against Germany in Sweden this summer. In fact, it was Peter who put the Danes through to the final by making the penalty save against Van Basten in a nail-biting finish to one of the best games in the tournament.

Why he couldn't have done the same for us in the FA Cup-tie against Southampton is another story and he can be assured that he will get a lot of stick for a long time on that one!

After signing Peter and going through the summer my main concern became the new ruling which allowed only four foreign players to be involved in a squad playing in a European competition. We had just signed two foreigners which, as it turned out, did not seem very sensible – the ruling came as quite a shock.

At the same time, I had no regrets because they are clearly going to enjoy brilliant careers at Old Trafford. What it did do, of course, was make me examine the entire squad which contained two Irishmen in Mal Donaghy and Denis Irwin, three Welshmen in Mark Hughes, Clayton Blackmore and Ryan Giggs, the Scot Brian McClair plus two new foreign players. On top of that, we had a lot of Scottish, Welsh and Irish boys coming along in the reserves, like Brian Carey and my son, Darren.

I hate to say it as a Scot but we were really short of Englishmen! Only two of the back four which had won the European Cup Winners' Cup were English. There was always Lee Martin, of course, but even with him fit again we were still one short in defence because my four foreign players had emerged as Schmeichel, Hughes, McClair and Kanchelskis. And that still left Irwin, Giggs and Blackmore out of the team.

So when we were on tour in Norway pre-season and I heard that Everton had made a bid for Paul Parker, I sat up and took notice. There seemed to be a problem because, despite the Everton interest, I heard he was also talking to Arsenal and Tottenham. I immediately got in touch with the Chairman who phoned QPR to ask if Paul would also talk to us. The reply came that he would. He met Arsenal and Spurs and came to us last, which always makes you think that your chances might not be very good.

However, the day he came to Old Trafford there were about three hundred supporters sitting in the stand. It was the middle of summer and quite an amazing sight. They just seemed to be watching the grass grow or perhaps, more usefully, willing it to grow. One of them shouted: 'Are you signing, Paul?' I'm sure that seeing fans simply breathing in the atmosphere in the close season reminded him that Manchester United are something special because straight away he shouted back: 'Yes, I'm signing'. I'm convinced it helped him make up his mind.

So with three new players in the bag and a European trophy on the sideboard I was feeling pretty pleased. We had lost Lee Sharpe with injury, but he was obviously going to be back in time, and in addition Ryan Giggs had broken through to become a major player. The thing about the 1991-92 season, though, was not so much winning the Rumbelows Cup or flying the flag as front runners in the League for most of the season, but how we came to grief at the end.

People say Leeds didn't so much win the Championship as have it handed to them on a plate. That's hardly fair to Leeds who, in my book, deserved their success. Nevertheless, we were on the slab for a detailed post-mortem and a searching examination of my management. The critics ignored the parts of the season when we were on fire. They gave us little credit for being in at the kill. The big question that had to be answered was what went wrong with us.

Possibly the most contentious part was team selection and the tactical changes I made in the course of the season. The thing that annoys me most of all is that I have made changes throughout my career to try and keep the edge on my teams and when you win things no-one mentions it at all. Then when things don't go quite to plan it's different and people latch on to the changes as a reason for losing. It's a symptom of the modern media, looking for the perverse aspect.

The pundits rarely spoke about the injuries we sustained towards the end or when we played four games in six days. I hardly came across criticism of the Football League for putting us into a position like that and I can't help wondering if their attitude would have been different had it been Liverpool experiencing those kind of difficulties.

Another aspect which didn't help us was our pitch. In October Johnny Giles wrote that he thought it would cost us the Championship and it was certainly an important factor.

All these things can be used as excuses but I don't want to hide behind our own deficiencies, and there are some hard facts for us to face. The area in which we failed was in our goal-scoring which dried up after New Year. I know statistics can be twisted but I think that the figures tell the whole story. Up to the turn of the year we scored 42 goals and in the second half we had dried up to 21. It was a crucial slump. You are not going to win as many games with goals so few and far between. You will either draw or lose.

I don't criticise any particular area of the team because we are all responsible. We share in the glory and we must share in the defeats and setbacks, too. We simply did not score enough goals as a team to even deserve winning the title. Overall we played quite well but I can certainly point to two or three performances where we let ourselves down.

The big one was the 4–1 defeat against Queens Park Rangers at Old Trafford on New Year's Day. It came as such a shock that people just had to find a reason and some of them invented their own. The most popular theory was that the players were drunk the night before because we were celebrating at a New Year's Eve party. Anyone who knows me will know that the allegation is ludicrous.

The other theory going the rounds was that people had seen the players in various pubs the day before the game. That was absolute nonsense as well because we were all together in a hotel, overnight. Apart from that, we have prided ourselves quite justifiably that since the early days we had sorted out the kind of high jinks described in Muhren's book and reported to me by Gordon Strachan.

We have come a long way from the time when Manchester United thought of themselves as a social club. We have got a good club now, not interested in the sideshow of soccer which, I concede, can easily happen in the English game. To suggest that the players would relapse into that torrid kind of behaviour was ridiculous.

If there was a reason for our unexpected collapse it would be found, in my view, on two fronts. Firstly, four or five players had had touches of flu for a couple of days. In fact, McClair, Hughes, Blackmore and Ince were loaded with it the night before the game. The second thing was that we made an absolutely ridiculous start to the game. We were two goals down in ten minutes and it doesn't matter who you are, that kind of set-back puts you in an almost impossible position.

I don't think the 5 p.m. kick-off, the unusual start chosen to fit in with TV, helped us or suited us. The fans certainly didn't like it and we had our lowest crowd of the season at Old Trafford, down 7,000 to 38,554.

These are all small things but if you are looking for reasons they are far more valid than gossip about players drinking. For my own part, my wife had arranged a surprise party in the hotel with a few friends down from Scotland because 31 December is my birthday. But come preparation for the game, I was more than ready. I wouldn't be so stupid as to leave myself short for a match after all the experience of life I have had.

None of this can fully explain the disappointment and even the following match, at home to Wimbledon, was another low point. We should have done better than 0-0. We had the beating of them but didn't finish them off. We also let ourselves down against Nottingham Forest in March when we lost 1-0 at the City Ground. We became locked in a draw sequence and approached the last few matches after conceding ground to Leeds. They had moved slowly but surely right on to our shoulder and they were ready to pounce when we destroyed ourselves with three successive defeats. We had not done particularly well with a 1-1 draw at Luton. We had taken an away point but at the same time there was no rhythm in our play. We moved into a lead we didn't deserve but still couldn't win the match. Luton played to avoid relegation and, looking back, it was an ominous result for us.

The next three games were shockers. The first was at home to Nottingham Forest. I have got to say it was a tremendously entertaining game and we didn't have much luck. We created a good number of scoring chances but if ever our deficiencies in front of goal were reflected in one match, this was it! Forest scored first but Brian McClair got a quick equaliser. He was the only player to keep our scoring momentum going. He needed more help, though, and didn't get it. Forest grabbed a winner near the end to leave me, not for the first time, examining our scoring. Or, more accurately, our lack of scoring.

The next match was lost 1-0 at West Ham, a black day and a bad result for us. We put the Londoners under a lot of pressure but were unable to score. I think our young players were fading, and it had become clear that they still have a lot to learn about operating in the last third of the field.

I have got to say, though, that I thought the West Ham performance was obscene in the sense of the effort they put into the match. I know there is a natural envy for Manchester United which often sees opponents raising their game, but considering that the Hammers were bottom of the League and already relegated it was almost criminal to see all that effort in a game that came too late to affect their own position. If I had been Billy Bonds I would have wanted to know why my players had not fought like that when their own future was at stake, and the issue was not simply one of Manchester United going for the Championship.

Their attitude was rather aptly summed up by a well-dressed, elderly man as he left the ground a few minutes before the end. He shouted to me quite pleasantly as he passed: 'Alex.' I turned towards him and he said: 'F*** you'. You ask yourself why people hate you like that. That night I experienced the bitterness that so many people undoubtedly feel towards Manchester United.

Certainly, we had not matched the fire and fury of the Hammers, perhaps hardly surprising considering that it was our fourth game in seven days and I suppose we had lost our poise and confidence. The final blow fell four days later when we crashed to a 2-0 defeat at Liverpool. The players gave everything but, in our hearts, I think we probably knew we had put Leeds in the driving seat. The match itself faded into insignificance compared with missing out on the Championship. Leeds had played earlier in the day and had won an amazing match against Sheffield United involving even an own-goal.

It was too late to question our rivals except to say they have my sincere congratulations on a marvellous achievement. People said that season was an ordinary and mediocre one. That's very unfair. The First Division was as hard to win as when Liverpool and Arsenal took the title. If you make mistakes you are punished and that's what happened to us. Leeds slipped up a few times themselves but kept their nerve to beat us fair and square.

When I reflect on the season as a whole, I look back and wonder whether I always picked the right team. From time to time in a 60-game season, you are bound to make the odd misjudgement. It has to be said, though, that sometimes people did not appreciate my strategy.

For instance, after the Southampton game I commented that Andrei Kanchelskis had been the match winner, as indeed he had after scoring our goal. But I knew his sharpness had gone and he knew himself that playing twice a week was too much for him. I left him out of the next match at Luton, brought him back for Forest and left him out at West Ham. So fans asked why did I drop the player I had described as a match winner. I had set myself up by my remark and people were angry because they could see the Championship slipping away. They were looking to slaughter the manager and they totally ignored the reason for resting Andrei.

Emlyn Hughes said I had bottled it. I had gone through purgatory for 18 months knocking the club into shape, and he had constantly assassinated me. Then when we won our European trophy he declared he had been wrong, just like that, as if all the other stuff didn't matter. Then here he was, changing tack again, to say I had messed things up.

I don't know anyone in the game who has any time for Emlyn Hughes. He is a disappointing character and it's sad that a man who has achieved so much in football can resort to gutter journalism. It's a disappointing reflection of modern football and there are others like him, players and managers turned critics, who stand on their heads for the sake of being controversial and who don't care who they hurt in the process.

Tommy Docherty, for instance, consistently slaughtered Neil Webb from the day he arrived. Then, when it suited him, he came out and blamed me for losing the Championship because I had dropped Webb. We all know about the Doc, though. He is what he is, a bitter old man.

But all these things cloud the issue. The underlying problem was the low scoring which became an increasing worry as the season wore on. It's never wise to apportion blame individually. A lot has been said in our dressing-room and in the confines of the club. The conclusion is that we intend to improve on that aspect of our play.

I put my best face on when the final blow fell at Anfield and it was just our rotten luck that it had to be against Liverpool, of all teams. Certainly, the disappointment was bitter but it should not be allowed to spoil the earlier part of the season which was notable for many things. We set out in splendid style and achieved my pre-season hope for a good start. So often in the past we have seemed to be hanging on to the coat-tails of Liverpool and Arsenal, simply giving ourselves too much to do in the later stages of the season.

We got the dream opening we wanted, beating Notts County in the first game and giving our supporters a taste of things to come with Andrei Kanchelskis. Our Ukrainian winger had a slight knock but still played well. Robson was also a bit of a gamble but it did not stop him scoring, along with Hughes. The opening team, which included Darren Ferguson wide on the left, lined up: Schmeichel, Irwin, Blackmore, Bruce, Ferguson, Parker, Robson, Ince, McClair, Hughes, Kanchelskis.

Gary Pallister had taken a pre-season strain and I held him back on the substitutes' bench for the first three games. Giggs was the other sub and there was no place for Neil Webb. Our three new players all showed up well and I was particularly impressed with the goalkeeper. If I was standing behind Schmeichel on the terraces I would be inclined to ask him to stand to one side so I could see the game. He's simply massive.

It was also obvious that there was a good spirit in the side, always a vital ingredient for a successful team. We had a winning result at Aston Villa in the next game with the help of a penalty from Bruce, the first time I had won at Villa Park. It was a steaming hot day at Everton in the following game and we didn't play well in the first half so I was happy to get a point from a goalless game.

It added up to seven points from nine to give us the opening I so badly wanted. For the next game I brought Webb in for his first start of the season and it produced an interesting response. He played with great enthusiasm and hunger. I was delighted. From the management point of view it's not easy to leave such a good player out of your team, but hands up to the lad, he showed me he was simply not prepared to be left out.

We were now embarked on an terrific run, playing some excellent stuff. We drew at home with Leeds, 1-1, conceding our first goal of the season which came from the kind of goalkeeping mistake which prompted me to say to Peter Schmeichel: 'Welcome to English football.' Lee Chapman had come round the back and the cross drifted over the goalkeeper's head to give him an easy header. If ever there was a game we should have won, that was it. We gave a really good performance, with Leeds contributing a good first half while the second half belonged to us. Certainly Leeds were delighted with a point and I was not too disappointed because we were showing superb spirit and character.

We were playing well and getting good results. Ryan Giggs was beginning to come into the game. I had brought him on against Leeds as substitute when Paul Ince was hurt after only 20 minutes and he showed us his wonderful talent. He really had them flapping on his runs. There was a lot of excitement that day even though we were without Kanchelskis who had been called up for a Russian qualifier for the European championships. It's one of the pitfalls of signing foreign players because other countries arrange fixtures outside the British system.

After the Leeds game we won at Wimbledon to start a run of five successive victories and confidence flooded through the team. You know it's a long season but I had wanted a good opening and the players had delivered. I could hardly have asked for more.

There was only one club in sight. I had looked on Arsenal as the big threat but they had got away to a poor beginning and Leeds were emerging as our rivals. When they played Arsenal I heard during the match that the Londoners had gone 2-0 up only for Leeds to fight back for a 2-2 draw. I thought at the time that it could be a significant result.

As the season progressed it became obvious that Leeds were the ones to watch. I was really enjoying it. It was clear we had a decent side. There was speed, imagination and tenacity. Bryan Robson was at a great peak and there was the excitement of Kanchelskis and Giggs on the wings. And, all the time, I knew we had Lee Sharpe to come, though it transpired that we never quite got him back in full flow. When a young lad misses pre-season training it takes a long time to catch up, particularly for a big, growing boy, like Sharpe.

We were not beaten until late October when we went down 3-2 at Sheffield Wednesday, perhaps significantly our 13th League game of the season. It was a terrific game of football but tiredness got to us in the end after a midweek European match in Madrid which left several players less than fully fit.

Steve Bruce was unbelievable with the way he played following an injection which left him sick at half-time. I had no complaints and I was proud of them as well as delighted with two goals from Brian McClair to give us a 2-1 lead. Jemson scored twice in the last ten minutes to give the home team their win. At this stage of the season we were launching into the various Cup competitions and of course fancied our chances based on our new found consistency in the League.

We kicked off well enough in defence of our European Cup Winners' Cup crown, drawing 0-0 against Athinaikos in Greece before winning the return, 2-0. One of the characteristics of European football, however, is that, just when you think you are doing well, the roof falls in.

Admittedly, we drew a tough one in Atletico Madrid but I hardly expected to lose 3-0 in Spain. Although Paulo Futre gave Atletico the lead after half an hour we controlled most of the game and played some enterprising football. Neil Webb headed against the post and I thought that a 1-0 defeat would give us a fair chance at Old Trafford. Then, miserably, we conceded two goals in the last couple of minutes. It was a great lesson for us. You must never take opponents of that quality for granted and 90 minutes means 90 minutes.

The defeat at Hillsborough three days later completed a black week, though happily we soon picked up again to notch some great victories. We moved steadily through the opening rounds of the Rumbelows Cup. We beat West Ham 2-1 and it should have been ten. We had a good 4-0 success against Coventry and we won at both Crystal Palace and Chelsea by convincing 3-1 scores.

Then we really cut loose to stun Oldham 6-3 at Boundary Park. The remarkable thing was that we missed half a dozen chances as well. To be fair, Oldham created quite a few opportunities themselves. I had to take Robson off at half-time and after bringing Giggs on we played a very positive 4-2-4 formation. Oldham pulled back to 2-1 but Denis Irwin, playing against his old club, made it 3-1. Oldham scored twice but we made scoring look easy with some great play. Talk about value

115

for money in that match. I knew from the way we started we were going to win and that was a regular feeling around that time.

The Super Cup was wedged in at this time and we beat Red Star 1-0 at Old Trafford. A lot of people said it was a hollow victory because instead of being played over two legs, home and away, it was made a single match event to avoid travelling to the troubles in Yugoslavia. Nevertheless, it was a triumph to come in 0-0 at half-time and some of the football we saw that night matched the performance against AC Milan when they beat us 3-2 in a pre-season friendly with all their Dutch stars. I had taken particular note of Marco Van Basten at that time because soon after coming to Old Trafford I had tried to sign him. I got Jesper Olsen to 'phone him because they had both played together at Ajax. It turned out he had already signed a pre-contract with Milan. Now against Red Star there was another star to drool over, Dejan Savicevic, a tremendous artist who gave a powerful performance against us that night.

Little did we know how events in Yugoslavia would develop so tragically and that they would be forced to withdraw from the European Championships. Red Star could easily have been three goals up at half-time but then we started to get a bit of shape in our team and I knew when McClair scored that we would win it.

I was able to bring on Giggs for a wee sniff of European atmosphere. He was emerging as an important player, so much so that a lot of fans wanted me to play him all the time. I resisted the temptation because I remembered my bitter experience at Aberdeen when I gave several youngsters their head and played them constantly. A few years later when they should have been at their peak they were all out of top football for one reason or another.

I was determined to handle Giggs the right way, regularly leaving him out to avoid over-taxing him. I wanted him for the end of the season and I also want him to be a star in ten years' time as well as now.

It was nice to win the Super Cup. Manchester United had never won it before and I think it's good to be able to look in the programme and see that at one time or another you have won all the trophies. We've got three now in Europe and a chance in the coming season to add the UEFA Cup to our honours list.

116

We turned back to the Rumbelows Cup to beat Oldham with goals from McClair and Kanchelskis to set us up for a quarter-final against Leeds. With only eight teams left it was hardly a great surprise but when we got the draw for the FA Cup a few days later it was certainly a shock to find us drawn at Elland Road again. It meant going to Leeds three times in the League and two Cup competitions in just over a fortnight.

Looking back, I think it was the peak of our season in terms of results and scoring. They were three absorbing games, demanding absolute concentration and energy. I know we were totally drained at the end of them and Leeds, I think, were the same. Their form was never that great afterwards but it affected us more because we won in both the FA and Rumbelows competitions. In addition to the actual combat on the field the crowd situation was also a worry. I am happy to say, though, that we got through without serious trouble. The games themselves were played with a great spirit, far different from the previous season. There had been a lot of heart-searching, particularly from Leeds, and I think Howard Wilkinson had analysed it well.

He had decided which was the way forward for his club. The game with Leeds of a year ago had been full of hatred. Our directors and their wives had even had coffee thrown over them, which should never happen. The encouraging thing is that Howard and I get on extremely well, as do the respective staffs. The players have taken the cue. They buried the hatchet and the three games were a credit to both clubs and to English football. You can get problems when you play the same people in a matter of days. I faced this in Scotland when feuds between Rangers and Celtic would linger because the top clubs met repeatedly.

Happily there was no crowd trouble either and I think everyone deserves a pat on the back. We drew the League game 1-1 with a goal from Webb, romped through the Rumbelows Cup 3-1 and knocked them out of the FA Cup 1-0. Yet we all enjoyed a drink together afterwards and that's where Howard has made a big contribution. He has made everyone, from players to fans, realise that Leeds are a big club again and can accept defeat with dignity.

The folly of winning both Cup-ties was brought home to roost towards the end of the season. There was one particular moment when

I thought: 'I don't know what is happening here.' It came in April when we drew 1-1 at home with Manchester City. We played stupidly. We were in front but didn't keep possession. I have got to say, though, that it was a period of great drama and great commitment as we battled against the draining effect of those Cup-ties. Publicly, I kept saying that we had the players to handle it but privately I was worried because we had freed Leeds for a clear run-in for the Championship while we continued to battle on three fronts.

Of the three games, the one I most wanted to win was the League fixture and, of course, we drew. We got in front but sat back and conceded a penalty kick when Gary Pallister crashed into Gary McAllister. If we had won against Leeds in December we would have gone seven points clear.

So we went to the turn of the year with everyone tipping us for the title while I was doing my best to keep feet on the ground, trying to be sensible so that no-one would get carried away. It's a great feeling when a team is in control and full of running, confident in their ability and giving certainly me total job satisfaction.

Somewhere along the line, though, the goals dried up. The pitch was bad and when players wanted to do something special with the ball it would bounce badly for them. We soon came unstuck in the FA Cup, but even here we managed to add to our fixture pile-up by drawing, in the fourth round, 0-0 at Southampton. It meant a replay and we went two goals down in the first 20 minutes. We fought back to draw 2-2 but then went out in the dreaded penalty shoot-out. Though naturally disappointed, I consoled myself with the thought that it was another competition less and I was also looking forward to the Rumbelows Cup semi-final which, with our challenge in the League, was quite enough on our plate.

The semi-finals against Middlesbrough turned out to be quite gruelling – goalless at Ayresome Park and we had to go into extra-time to win 2-1 at Old Trafford.

Our best performances, though, were happening away from Old Trafford. Even though the goals were thinning, excitement started to build up and the support really got behind the team, sensing the title possibilities and determined to join the party.

So it was a great disappointment how it all turned out. We still have to be pleased with the overall performance and the players can feel satisfied that they are at the right club. One thing that emerged crystal clear was that Manchester United must never allow anyone, ever again, to force them to play four games in seven days when their main League rivals were resting, 35 miles away.

We would have been better off refusing to play, conceding the points and paying a heavy fine. Teams should not be penalised for success and great credit is due to Howard Wilkinson who recognised that that was the weakness in our pack of cards. In fact, it was their joker.

We also started with injuries at a bad time and we went into those four crucial games without Robson, Parker or Ince. People said we particularly missed Robson but that is only half-true. I certainly think we would have done the business better with the captain in the team. In ordinary circumstances we now have a team quite capable of performing without him. We don't depend on him so much these days and we have won plenty of games without our Captain Marvel.

At the same time, when the pressure was applied and nerves were jangling, he is the one man who could have steadied the ship. Deep down, a lot of players, and myself, wanted to win the League for Bryan because he's a man who, for a decade, worked his tripe off for the club. He has had broken limbs, a shoulder injury, hamstring injuries – all kinds of knocks yet the fire still burns.

Robson, apart from the football side which is there for everyone to examine and admire in his record, is a man's man. He's a fair-minded lad who can see the other side of an argument. He can accept criticism. He can accept the way life goes but he still bubbles when it matters on the football field. I don't think United could get a more influential player. Hopefully they will again, and even more hopefully, in my time, because his value at Old Trafford has been unbelievable. If Ron Atkinson had done nothing else, he would have earned his keep at United by bringing him here. Bryan has been a brilliant player for the club and I can say now that looking to this season, I have got Robson in my team. He may not be able to play 60 games but if I get 30 from him I will be satisfied because I know his performances will be of value and influence.

119

Even when he wasn't playing last season, he travelled with us to games and still made a contribution. Unhappily, Robson had been hurt at Norwich after repeatedly defying medical advice to rest a damaged shin which affected his calf muscle. He missed the Rumbelows Cup final and he only played in the final game of the decisive run that saw us fail to win the title. Before that fatal spell of four games in a week, only four teams had beaten us all season. That one week of agony was a killer and it prevented us from having the best season in the history of the club.

I have got to admit, though, that I had been worried for some time about the frequency of drawn games. As early as February, for instance, we had played Sheffield Wednesday off the park at Old Trafford but were held to a 1-1 draw and that was a scenario to be repeated too often. We still managed to get some good results, of course, such as Sheffield United and Norwich away when Robson was bang on form and I said to myself: 'This is a Championship team.'

I wonder now whether it was the 1-1 draw with Manchester City at Old Trafford that started our slide in the League. We were in total control of that game, and after Giggs had scored I was just waiting for a second goal to go in. Then Neil Pointon got himself sent off. The lad had a rush of blood. People say it was a bad tackle by Giggs but I've watched it on video since and there was nothing wrong with it. It was enough, though, for Pointon to lose his temper and retaliate. He got sent off and, far from that weakening City, it was us who cracked. We went stupid for five minutes and Bruce dived in to give a penalty away. I can still see him thinking: 'What have I done here?' From then on we were lucky to pick up a point because City could so easily have beaten us.

The next game was the Rumbelows final against Nottingham Forest and naturally we put the derby and the Championship out of our minds to make sure of at least one trophy. We went into the game very relaxed. I decided to change the normal preparation and we simply went down to London the day before because we had important League fixtures coming up. There was to be no celebration afterwards, and we came back on the train before meeting up for a quiet evening meal with our families.

I felt confident about beating Forest. I had watched them play in the Zenith Cup final and had picked up one or two things. They had also beaten us in the League and I knew how important Clough and Keane were to their team. We worked out a strategy to counter them and, in the main, we controlled the match very well. In fact, we should have won more easily than the score suggested. McClair scored our goal, a good move involving Pallister and Giggs.

The euphoria of winning the League Cup competition had hardly died down when we were launched into our black period. A few days before the final we had decided to let Mark Robins have a cartilage operation because we had everyone, apart from Robson, fit. Then people started to go down like ninepins. It was as if fate was saying, 'Sorry, but you will have to wait another year for the Championship.' Ince was injured against Southampton, Parker was hurt at Luton and Lee Martin found an old injury flaring again. Wallace and Beardsmore were even injured in a reserve game.

So, suddenly we were scrambling about, forced to change the team around. All credit to the players in many respects. Against Forest at home, for instance, we annihilated them. They didn't get a corner kick but our luck generally seemed to be out because we lost 2-1. I came out after the match to meet the media quite stunned, though I thought I handled the situation well. You wouldn't have thought so reading a couple of the papers the next day. There was more of this 'Fergie Fury' which I get so often if I am at all critical. It certainly annoyed me in this instance because it wasn't true. One reporter even wrote on Tuesday that I had stormed out. He wasn't even at the match and it was disappointing because his paper is a step up from the seamy tabloids. What chance have you if the better papers let you down like that?

Injuries and the media were not the only problems at this point. I also had a complication with Neil Webb which he now probably wishes had never happened because he was forced to face the reality of how important I consider Manchester United to be in the scheme of things.

The situation arose following a goalless game with Wimbledon and, knowing the injuries I had, any player with the slightest knock was withdrawn from the international fixtures which were coming up.

121

I considered I simply could not afford nine players away on international duty. Our club had waited 25 years for the holy Championship grail and trying to secure it deserved everyone's loyalty and commitment, the same commitment that has made people devote their lives to us and seen them spend fortunes following us, even at the expense of ruining family life. Manchester United have taken over so many lives and you are taking liberties if you meddle with their loyalty.

I have always promised international team managers that in the big games I will not let them down. However, there are some ridiculous friendly fixtures arranged these days. We have seen teams going to Saudi Arabia, Bahrain, New Zealand, Australia, America and, if they could, I'm sure they would like a trip to Timbuktu. I just wonder sometimes whether the FA councillors look to these jaunts as junkets in return for the time and effort they put into the game. That type of fixture is useless for clubs and even, I suggest, for the national team managers because they rarely get all the players they want. It became clear that Graham Taylor took umbrage when I withdrew Webb from the squad due to go to Czechoslovakia. The Press had a field day, hinting at the England manager's anger with United and I don't see it as a coincidence that Gary Pallister and Paul Parker have since been bummed right out of the picture and were not considered for the European Championships in the summer. What Parker was doing at home when England were crying out for a right-back in Sweden, I'll never know.

Graham Taylor and I had a few angry words but I refuse to accept criticism for doing my best for Manchester United. I can do without that kind of nonsense. I've a job to do, and so has he, but, for heaven's sake, fancy organising friendly games at that time of the year.

In particular I take great exception to whoever arranged a friendly international on 29 April which prevented us from being able to play a midweek match. I believe it had as much to do with us losing the Championship as anything. England, or any of the other national bodies for that matter, have no excuse for coming up with silly fixtures for that time of year.

The upshot was that Neil chose to inform the England manager that he was actually fit and that he was only withdrawn on my

122

instructions. I felt he was totally out of order and I did not like the attempts made by Graham Taylor to inform the Press about United's role in the withdrawal of players.

The facts were that Pallister had been bothered by his back, Ince was injured from the Wimbledon game and Parker was being troubled by his recurring hamstring strain. Sharpe was not fully back in action. So what do you do in that kind of situation? I withdrew Webb as well because in addition to our England internationals, we had other players being called up for international duty. I got a more sympathetic response from some of the other countries. I phoned Maurice Setters to pull out Denis Irwin and he immediately said that they didn't expect to have him anyway because of our important games coming up. It was great to find that kind of understanding. I've told them all that I'll be there with my players for the key competition games.

I was still inclined to pick Neil but he had to be taught a lesson to ram home how important Manchester United is to me, to the supporters and everyone else committed to the club. He knew he was in the wrong and after a couple of weeks he apologised. By the time of the Rumbelows final I considered he deserved to come back. He had turned in some good performances in the earlier rounds and played his part getting us to Wembley, so I made him one of the substitutes.

He stayed as sub for the following game against Southampton and came on to do quite well, though not by his standards, and I was left with the dilemma of wondering whether the whole business had affected him. He was feeling some remorse and it may have left him unable to get his game back. It more or less ended the season for Neil and at an unfortunate time for us.

At a time like that you want players to step forward and say 'Let me carry the banner' … like Robson and Ince playing in the do-or-die match at Liverpool despite carrying injuries. That tells you a lot about their courage and defiance. They showed their team-mates, myself and the supporters that they were not going to be shot down without a fight. That's why I never took them off, even though in the last 20 minutes their legs had gone and they were playing from memory. I knew by then that the inevitable had happened and we had lost the League.

One of the depressing aspects was that we had all thought Sheffield United were going to win or draw against Leeds in the game played just before we kicked off at Anfield. I never expected a Sheffield team which was in good form to lose three goals at home and when you saw the kind of goals they were you realised that when your luck is in, it's in and when it's out you have no chance.

We battled well at Anfield. We applied a lot of pressure on them and dominated, but went down 2-0. Ronnie Moran said afterwards that it had been their best performance for months. At least we showed courage and pride. We didn't resort to any bad tackles. I told our players at half-time that whatever happened I didn't want anyone wearing our colours to lose their dignity. I wanted to hold our heads high. Liverpool were playing in a Cup-final two weeks later, but we didn't try to cash in on that by resorting to anything unduly physical.

We set out to try and win the League the way we wanted to win it or not at all.

SEASON 1991-92
FIRST DIVISION

	P	W	D	L	F	A	PTS
Leeds United	42	22	16	4	74	37	82
MANCHESTER UNITED	42	21	15	6	63	33	78
Sheffield Wednesday	42	21	12	9	62	49	75
Arsenal	42	19	15	8	81	46	72
Manchester City	42	20	10	12	61	48	70
Liverpool	42	16	16	10	47	40	64
Aston Villa	42	17	9	16	48	44	60
Nottingham Forest	42	16	11	15	60	58	59
Sheffield United	42	16	9	17	65	63	57
Crystal Palace	42	14	15	13	53	61	57
Queens Park Rangers	42	12	18	12	48	47	54
Everton	42	13	14	15	52	51	53
Wimbledon	42	13	14	15	53	53	53
Chelsea	42	13	14	15	50	60	53
Tottenham Hotspur	42	15	7	20	58	63	52
Southampton	42	14	10	18	39	55	52
Oldham Athletic	42	14	9	19	63	67	51
Norwich City	42	11	12	19	47	63	45
Coventry City	42	11	11	20	35	44	44
Luton Town	42	10	12	20	38	71	42
Notts County	42	10	10	22	40	62	40
West Ham Utd	42	9	11	22	37	59	38

APPEARANCES

	League	Rumbelows Cup	ECWC	FA Cup	Total
Brian McClair	41(1)	8	4	3	56(1)
Peter Schmeichel	40	6	3	3	52
Mark Hughes	38(1)	6	4	2(1)	50(2)
Gary Pallister	37(3)	8	3(1)	3	51(4)
Denis Irwin	37(1)	7	2	3	49(1)
Steve Bruce	37	7	4	1	49
Ryan Giggs	32(6)	6(2)	0	2(1)	40(9)
Paul Ince	31(2)	6(1)	3	3	43(3)
Neil Webb	29(2)	6	3	3	41(2)
Andrei Kanchelskis	28(6)	4	0	2	34(6)
Bryan Robson	26(1)	5(1)	3	2	36(2)
Paul Parker	24(2)	6	2	3	35(2)
Clayton Blackmore	19(14)	4(1)	0	1	24(15)
Mal Donaghy	16(4)	3(1)	0	2	21(5)
Mike Phelan	14(4)	2(1)	4	0	20(5)
Lee Sharpe	8(6)	1(3)	0	0(1)	9(10)
Darren Ferguson	2(2)	0	0	0	2(2)
Gary Walsh	2	1	0	0	3
Mark Robins	1(1)	0(3)	2(1)	0	3(5)
Lee Martin	0(1)	1	1(2)	0	2(3)
Ian Wilkinson	0	1	0	0	1
Russell Beardsmore	0	0	1(2)	0	1(2)
Danny Wallace	0	0	1(1)	0	1(1)

GOALSCORERS

	League	Rumbelows Cup	ECWC	FA Cup	Total
Brian McClair	18	4	1	1	24
Mark Hughes	11	0	2	1	14
Steve Bruce	5(3)	1	0	0	6(3)
Andrei Kanchelskis	5	2	0	1	8
Ryan Giggs	4	3	0	0	7
Denis Irwin	4	0	0	0	4
Bryan Robson	4	1	0	0	5
Clayton Blackmore	3(1)	1	0	0	4(1)
Paul Ince	3	0	0	0	3
Neil Webb	3	0	0	0	3
Lee Sharpe	1	1	0	0	2
Mark Robins	0	2	0	0	2
Gary Pallister	1	0	0	0	1
Own Goal	1	0	0	0	1
Total	63(4)	15	3	3	84(4)

* Bracketed figures denote penalties

EUROPEAN CUP WINNERS' CUP

Round 1/1	Athinaikos	(A)	D	0-0
Round 1/2	Athinaikos	(H)	W	2-0 (aet)
Round 2/1	Atletico Madrid	(A)	L	0-3
Round 2/2	Atletico Madrid	(H)	D	1-1

FA CUP

Round 3	Leeds United	(A)	W	1-0
Round 4	Southampton	(A)	D	0-0
Replay	Southampton	(H)	L	2-2 (2-4 pens aet)

LEAGUE CUP

Round 2/1	Cambridge Utd	(H)	W	3-0
Round 2/2	Cambridge Utd	(A)	D	1-1
Round 3	Portsmouth	(H)	W	3-1
Round 4	Oldham Athletic	(H)	W	2-0
Round 5	Leeds United	(A)	W	3-1
Semi-final/1	Middlesbrough	(A)	D	0-0
Semi-final/2	Middlesbrough	(H)	W	2-1 (aet)
Final	Nottingham Forest	Wembley	W	1-0

EUROPEAN SUPER CUP

Red Star Belgrade	(H)	W	1-0

(Scorer: McClair)

Chapter Eight

THE GRAND OLD MAN

Probably my most controversial decision as I juggled my resources during the closing stages of the 1991-92 season's Championship bid was dropping Mark Hughes. After a great deal of deliberation I left him out of the home game against Nottingham Forest following a ten-match run without a goal from him.

The essence of a striker, the meat of his game, is scoring goals and I simply had to look closely at Mark at a couple of stages. A great deal is required of the men up front, of course, and even in a dry run they can still be more than worth their place for what they contribute to the team in terms of leading the line and creating play for those around them. Mark has a great many qualities, but sooner or later you have got to assess the scoring in general and the centre-forward's goals in particular.

I had this kind of situation with Mark McGhee at Aberdeen when he went 23 games without scoring. We didn't have the kind of options we enjoy at Old Trafford either! So I persevered with him for what seemed an eternity without a goal. I was close to leaving him out in the match prior to a big European game in order to try someone else, but in the end gave him one last chance, in the meantime working on his confidence and trying all ways to give him a boost.

It didn't work because he had a shocker against Morton – such a bad game, totally lacking in confidence – so that I just could not risk him against Hamburg. I put it to him: 'How long do I wait?' My patience had run out, and I chose him as a substitute. The game came and we were doing no better. Indeed it was a lot worse and we were 3-0 down with half an hour to go. I brought him on and he promptly proceeded to score an absolutely magnificent goal.

Later I asked him what his thoughts had been and how he had handled being dropped. He explained that the minute he knew I had left him out he felt relaxed and the stress had gone. It was a bit like that for the final game of the 1991-92 season against Spurs at Old Trafford when we knew we had lost the League title and we scored three goals for the first time for months.

There are people who work in stress management and the pressure comes in a variety of ways. The reaction varies, too, depending on temperament and the ability to keep things in perspective. What part, for instance, did stress play in the retirement of Kenny Dalglish from Liverpool? And was bottled-up emotion involved in the recent heart illness of Graeme Souness?

Mark McGhee was under stress. The moment it was lifted off him it was eased and he began to express himself with confidence again. You look at 'Sparky' and he is regarded as a confident, flamboyant character, but he is far from it. Appearances are deceptive because off the field Mark is an unassuming kind of bloke who likes the quiet life. On the field he seems to use the stage as an outlet for the deeper emotions he normally hides. It's as if part of him is bursting to get out and his spectacular goals and fierce commitment represent the buried personality coming out.

When I omitted him against Forest he had been in a valley of bad form and sometimes the only way up the other side is a break from the action to ease the expectation. I made him a substitute and I believe it was the best thing that could have happened to him. The crowd were chanting his name as he sat on the bench, reinforcing that belief within Mark concerning his ability and self-respect. For when I brought him on he used those fleeting minutes to give everything and he looked a different player.

Of course there was also bound to have been an element of hitting back at me for giving him the shock treatment, but that is OK. You want players who respond with the bit between their teeth. You can never leave your character in the dressing-room and Mark showed us his in adversity.

In terms of confidence, losing and regaining it, we have discussed it at length at the club and I have been turning over in my mind for some time the idea that we should get an analyst in to help players who suddenly start to struggle. I remember Spurs trying it once though, with a sports psychologist, and the minute he left the club he was writing a book about his experiences. The last thing you want is someone parading the personal problems of your players in print. In terms of stress that could send you off the scale! So I am always wary about bringing outsiders into my club. At the same time I accept that there is an increasing need to examine this area.

Overall, of course, there is no doubting the value of Mark Hughes. He is one of the few players people come specially to watch, one of the few players who are real individuals. The way football has changed, with its emphasis on team spirit and organisation, has meant that some managers and coaches have been able to make careers without any great talent except the ability to organise. They have bypassed what I would consider to be more important qualities like tactical planning and motivation.

Even at the highest level there are managers who have created reasonably successful teams simply as organisers insisting on discipline and spirit. It's a drift to the American concept of rah-rah-rah where team play is dominant, but in my view that approach only gets you so far, never all the way to the top, and it begs the question of what you are doing to entertain people. Such teams are parasites, living off the backs of those who try to foster real ability and encourage players to express themselves.

So there are still players who relate to their own game and who like to perform on a stage simply because it is a stage and they are up there under the spotlight. Paul Gascoigne plays like that, and whatever you may think about his antics, he certainly puts bums on seats and brings people to football.

I remember an interesting game between Spurs and Leeds when David Batty was given the job of marking Gascoigne. The strange thing was that Leeds were on top, but Gascoigne was in control of his shadow. It was no reflection on Batty who in fact had a good game, but it still didn't stop Gascoigne teasing Leeds and producing his full bag of tricks. Of course he overdid it, which is his weakness, and getting him to strike the right balance will undoubtedly send the coach's stress level shooting up!

The bottom line for a player like Gascoigne or an individual like our own Mark Hughes is to examine what he delivers for the team. For a striker you have to examine the number of goals and the 'assists' he provides. If you relate this to Sparky he won the European Cup Winners' Cup for us with his two goals, he scored twice to keep us alive in the first game of the FA Cup final against Crystal Palace and in the 1991-92 season it was his goal which saw us knock Leeds out of the FA Cup.

That is just a small sample of his importance to Manchester United and it makes you reluctant to leave him out of the team even when you know he is playing badly and the goals have deserted him.

Graham Taylor, the England manager, says managers should not fall in love with their players. I take his point because love is blind, but every team boss has a wee affection for those players who give everything. To my mind there is nothing wrong with having that kind of warmth and respect for the guys you watch coming off knowing they have nothing left to give because they have given it all. I always maintain that after a match if every player can look round the dressing-room and say each one has given as much as himself then you can be satisfied you have a proper team.

Graham Taylor's point, of course is that you must not let emotion cloud a critical assessment because the time always comes for a player when the legs don't function quite the same and he is on the far side of the slope. Players eventually move into a grey area you are not quite sure about. I have faced it many times and have had to ask myself whether the time has come for a change. At Old Trafford in a relatively short space of time the careers of good players like Kevin Moran, Arthur Albiston, Norman Whiteside, Jesper Olsen and Gordon Strachan have all posed particular problems over timing. I had to examine how they were performing in matches, look at them in training and count up how many games they were playing and how many they were missing with injury. You can easily make a mistake, but what you must not do as a manager is worry. You have to make the decision and then move on to your next success, or, of course, to your next mistake!

All this did not stop supporters asking me: 'How can you leave Mark Hughes out of such an important game on the run-in for the Championship?'

It wasn't of course an overnight decision or a sudden whim. I had gone through all the procedures that I had followed in my previous management with Mark McGhee. I had sat down with Mark and tried to find out whether there was anything bothering him away from the club, with his family for instance. I made it clear that I was looking to help him in the hope of discovering the little one per cent extra needed to see him in full flow again. There was nothing obvious. So remembering earlier in the season when I had left him out of an FA Cup-tie at Southampton and his storming response, I decided on the shock treatment. The other important aspect was that it might also indicate how much we rely on him in other areas of the game.

I had applied this strategy to other players of course. I left out Brian McClair against Luton until bringing him on as a substitute when he grabbed two goals in half an hour. How people react is of course a measure of them and in the case of McClair it was very obvious: 'Don't dare drop me again.'

It begs the question of why couldn't he have done it without being dropped, but that's perhaps another story and we are all human, I guess. But certainly I was looking for that kind of reply when I dropped Mark and, to be fair to him, I got it. Unhappily, when I brought him back the following game it was the West Ham debacle and the whole team were struggling. Liverpool applied the *coup de grace* and it was all over as far as the Championship was concerned. Mark still had the last word, scoring twice in the 3-1 win against Spurs in the final match of the season.

The relationship between a manager and his players is obviously a tricky and delicate one. Some would say that it is the partnership between a manager and his assistant that is the most important relationship at a club. For me, though, it is the working partnership between manager and chairman which is the vital key.

When I first started as a manager I was impulsive and impetuous. I wanted to do things without telling or referring to anyone else. As you get experience – and I have had 18 years as a manager now – the edges get knocked off and you are not as vulnerable either.

131

I have been fortunate in that I worked for a remarkable chairman at Aberdeen, Dick Donald, and we developed a good understanding. Considering Manchester United are a vastly bigger club and the chairman is also chief executive, I consider I have been doubly fortunate to have Martin Edwards as chairman.

The most important thing is that there should be a mutual respect and that is exactly what exists between us. Martin has never once queried or spoken to me about the operational side of team management. It certainly wasn't like that in my very early days. I recall at the end of one season in Scotland, when I presented my list of players available for free transfer to the board, one of the directors objected. He reckoned one of the players I had on my list was a future international and would prove to be one of the best players Scotland had ever had. I said that was his opinion, to which he was entitled, but that as far as I was concerned the player had no chance of making it. It was a ridiculous situation because matters like that must be left to the manager. There has to be trust in his judgement, or why appoint him?

Martin has never questioned anything like that. The only occasion he gave me some advice was when I was having a bad time and he asked me if I minded him saying something. Of course I said I didn't, all the time wondering what was coming next! All he said, in fact, was that I was doing too much, taking on too many jobs and that I should delegate more.

I thought about it and concluded he was absolutely right. I took his advice. I spread the load far wider and it has helped me a lot. The help came at an important time, too, in the sense that as you get older, energies are not the same and it is important to concentrate on the really important aspects of the job.

When I first came down to England I was totally involved in the school of excellence I had instigated and because we had only four scouts operating in the Manchester area I was going to games nearly every night of the week. Then, of course, there were the insatiable demands of supporter functions.

It is doubly important at a club the size of Manchester United to delegate and I am only on the periphery of all the extraneous things now. I know the system is working and that is all I need to know. I'm only interested in the results of it all so that I can be fresher for the things I will be judged by.

It was good advice the Chairman gave me because the kind of pressure I am subjected to at Manchester United just did not happen to me at Aberdeen which was a tight little club, easily controlled. In fact we didn't even have board meetings as such. There were only three directors and the Chairman simply used to drop in at lunchtime for a sandwich, discuss a few things and that was it, the business was done.

United have a wide range of directors and need that kind of input. We have a solicitor in Maurice Watkins, businessmen like Michael Edelson and Amer Midani, Les Olive, who has been at the club man and boy, first as a junior player and then as secretary, and then of course Bobby Charlton, a great player and now a wonderful ambassador for the club. I must not forget either Michael Knighton and Nigel Burrows, neither of whom is with us any more.

The decision to make Les Olive a director was not only a nice gesture but a far-sighted one. I rate him a really important contributor on the board. He will not vote necessarily with popular opinion but for what he thinks is right for the club. Because of his long service as an administrator he is an expert on the interpretation of rules and regulations. Basically, he is the director responsible for the reserve team and he watches a lot of youth football. He's a great credit to the club, a smashing man. He provides a good mix of personalities.

Amer Midani is not at the club as much he as would like because of his business affairs abroad. Perhaps one day the situation will improve and enable him to spend more time in this country. Amer is a mannerly man with a well established interest in Manchester's sporting scene after supporting basketball for many years. I hope it will not be very long before he can contribute once more in this country.

There is a great spirit in the boardroom. Half the time they joke and wind each other up, which tells you that they get on and have a good relationship. I have not been at a board meeting yet where there has been any real acrimony, argument yes, but then there have been plenty of contentious issues. The directors have had to consider controversial problems like the Premier League, the development of the Stretford End, the size of the stadium, the pricing structure and, of course, always, the buying and selling of players.

Hand on heart, though, I have never known a happier board and I hope it stays that way. It's essential for a manager to know he has the directors behind him. For instance, when I was under pressure there was never any hostile atmosphere at our meetings. When it came to the manager's report, there was none of this hushed silence when they listen to you but don't really hear what you are saying, if you know what I mean.

It's an open atmosphere which I feel is liberating and gives me the freedom to express myself at the board meetings. They ask me my opinion, they give me a vote and there is an acceptance of my contribution, which is healthy and encouraging. It's good to know you can put a view which will be accepted without rancour. I can't look at any one director and say he doesn't support me.

We have a good rapport. The favourite line when I want to buy a player is to tell them that it's the last piece of the jigsaw, and, as Mike Edelson is fond of reminding me, it's the biggest jigsaw in the world. Michael is the man who loves to wind me up. Before big games he has a habit of coming up to me and saying: 'I don't want to panic you, but you know this is the most important match the club have ever played.' Then he walks away chuckling. On the more serious side he has been responsible for forming a medical committee and financing youth development. He is a 'doer' all right.

The only sad note on the board is the rough ride the chairman gets from the public. I've known Martin Edwards for six years and it's obvious there is a resentment towards him from the crowd. He gets some terrible abuse if he goes out on to the pitch to make a presentation or something like that. I asked him why he continued to put himself in the firing line like that when he knew he would inevitably get some stick and he simply replied: 'I've got to, haven't I?' He shows courage facing up to that part of it because they do really give him a hard time.

Every now and again a player will undeservedly come in for that kind of treatment. They tell me young Johnny Aston suffered from fans who were always on his back. There is a perverse streak in a football crowd when they pick on somebody they don't fancy. Martin probably regrets a couple of decisions he has taken over the years which have not endeared him to the support and it's built up from there. Perhaps the fact that he became the majority shareholder and, in effect, the owner of Manchester United was the starting point. Ordinary punters will find it difficult to look on Martin as one of them. Then there is the fact that his father had money and Martin inherited not only wealth but control of the club. Envy can be a powerful force in human nature. On top of all this, of course, he is chief executive, getting paid. Somebody has to do that job and Martin is qualified to do it. It's not a free ride either. He works hard but if he makes a mistake it only adds to his problem and the mountain gets bigger.

It's a difficult one to climb. People say winning the Championship will win the fans over but he doesn't think so. My own view is that he will not win until people can sum up his contribution over a long period and put it into proper perspective. He has supported all his managers and he has certainly given me loyal backing. He has made sure money has been provided which I consider fulfils his main obligation to the supporters. He has ensured we have the best possible team out on the park and he deserves more credit for that than the crowd seem prepared to give him.

Projects like setting up schools of excellence and bringing in the extra physiotherapist we now have at the club all cost money but the chairman doesn't quibble. It's just a pity the fans are not in a position to appreciate how thoroughly supportive he is. He deserves more consideration. It may not be personally very encouraging for him, but he may be like some of the great poets who were not recognised until they were dead. You can't draw much comfort from that epitaph but it's more than the crowd are allowing him! Certainly at the end of the day you wonder whether the next chairman will be as good for the managers at Manchester United.

Then we have a director who, in contrast to Martin, can do no wrong. Bobby Charlton is a great hero and, of course, he enjoys the advantage of having performed great deeds out on the pitch. He understands the complexities of a manager's job and it's a big help when you have got someone like him who has been a player as well as a manager and who knows the club inside out. His support for me in the boardroom has been brilliant. Being a real football man like Les

Olive, it's like having a good half-back line behind you. The amazing thing is his incredible shyness. I remember going with him to watch Mark Hughes play for Barcelona. It was lovely to see him relaxed and dropping his shyness. As a player, he was one of those people I talked about earlier who used his personality on the football stage and found it easier to express himself that way. On this particular occasion, Barcelona lost to Dundee United and the crowd were calling for the head of Terry Venables who was the manager. There were thousands of fans outside and Bobby and I were standing in a doorway, waiting and hoping for the crowd to disperse. We must have been trapped there for half an hour with supporters chanting for Terry's blood. It was all a bit frightening but they suddenly recognised Bobby and the mood changed instantly. They went wild with enthusiasm for him and I immediately jumped on the bandwagon. I shouted: 'I'm with Bobby', and we got away safely. He is one of those figures who, no matter where they go in the world, are always recognised.

Maurice Watkins is a cool customer who doesn't panic. When we went to London for the FA enquiry into the Arsenal fracas and we got the result, Martin and I were fuming. The Highbury people, Dennis Hill-Wood and George Graham, were going off their heads as well but Arsenal's solicitor and Maurice were as cool as cucumbers. You need a man like that on the board as well.

Nigel Burrows ran into financial problems which have since seen him resign from the board. It's a pity because he represented and reflected the attitude of the supporters. He was always prepared to speak up for the ordinary fan. He was good in his work for the club, supported every team and travelled all over with us.

Michael Knighton was the odd one out on the board, distanced by his controversial attempt to buy the club and the hullaballoo that followed. He came in and out of the club but had little impact because the chemistry was not right. He was always mannerly and he always supported me but his resignation was probably best under the circumstances. There was always a strain.

Sir Matt Busby is now the President of Manchester United and as such is no longer a member of the board. I still include him, though, in any discussion of the hierarchy at Old Trafford because of what he did in his day and the influence he still has. He achieved everything and must feel at peace with himself. He doesn't need to compete any more, of course, and at 83 he is in the twilight of his years and entitled to some peace and quiet. I've looked at his record and it is quite evident that he made the club into the institution we know today.

Looking back over the years, though, I'm encouraged to think that my own career at Old Trafford has at least started to go down a similar road. His first trophy was the FA Cup and a few seasons later he won the League championship after finishing second a few times. Well, I've won the FA Cup and finished League runners-up twice now. Europe is another avenue Sir Matt took with distinction and another hurdle which I have overcome. Sir Matt sprouted the Busby Babes and I'm certainly trying my utmost to create our own young players again. When you study his career you can see his plans unfolding. It's marvellous to behold. He wasn't just living from day to day—he had an overall strategy which, by 1955, saw him produce a brilliant team only to see it destroyed in the Munich air crash three years later, still to reach its peak. He had bought players but only to add to a nucleus of talent he had found and nurtured.

Liverpool have tended to buy their players and, to their credit, have bought brilliantly but I think Sir Matt got more satisfaction through producing his own. I certainly get a bigger thrill from seeing a schoolboy go all the way to the top. Matt developed gems like Bobby Charlton and George Best but it's interesting to note that he bought for positions where he knew he had to be particularly strong. He bought one or two goalkeepers in his time and he went to the transfer market for goal-scorers like Tommy Taylor and Denis Law. There was a pattern to his method, always a similar mix of bought and home-made to his teams.

My aim, with Sir Matt very much in mind, is to maintain the club's reputation and tradition, do my utmost to win a trophy every year and do my best. You can never come to a club and think you can change what has been built. It is Matt Busby's club and there has been talk over the years about living in his shadow. But if managers who preceded me felt that way then they have, perhaps, not looked at the job the right way. In fairness, I had a lot of success at Aberdeen so it was perhaps slightly different for me. I didn't come feeling I had to prove myself in the way others may have felt.

What I had to do was prove to myself that I can handle a club as big as Manchester United as opposed to running a smaller club like Aberdeen. It was a personal challenge rather than a worldly one. When I came down to England, the first thing I asked myself was whether I had any envy for Matt Busby. I can honestly say that it was not a problem for me. I found him a wonderful and incredible man. People talk about his great memory, recalling names after one meeting, but you are talking about a man of substance, character and charisma.

I love to listen to Nobby Stiles describing how Matt dropped him a couple of times from the team. It was done with great style. Nobby recalls how he was summoned to his office to be greeted with a friendly enquiry about how he was getting on. Nobby replied: 'Fine, thank you, Boss.' Matt then asked him if he thought he was playing as well as he could and when Nobby found himself admitting that he could do better Matt jumped straight in with the decision: 'Well then, I think you could be doing with a wee rest .'

Nobby left the office kicking himself as he realised he had helped the manager to drop him. He made up his mind that it wouldn't happen like that again if the occasion should arise. He vowed he would stick up for himself. Of course, the time arrived when, once more, he was summoned. 'How are you, son, and how do you think you are playing?' This time Nobby was prepared. 'Well, how do *you* think I'm playing, Boss?' Matt explained that he thought Nobby could play better and didn't he agree? Nobby was forced to admit that he could, probably, do better and Matt was straight in again: 'Yes, I thought so.' Nobby had dropped himself once more.

Matt was shrewd all right, as he demonstrated in another story told to me by Jimmy Ryan. He and John Fitzpatrick were disappointed when they found that some of their team-mates had got bigger bonuses after winning the Championship in 1967. Fitzpatrick was not at all happy and kept on about what he was going to tell the Old Man and how he wasn't going to stand for it. He asked Jimmy if he would come with him to see the Boss and Jimmy reluctantly agreed. John saw his chance when they were away on tour and got hold of his friend and convinced him the time was right. They went to the manager's room and knocked at the door.

'Come in, boys, how are you doing and what can I do for you?' said Matt. Up spoke John Fitzpatrick: 'Go on, Jimmy, tell him.' Jimmy much abashed, stammered out their grievance. Sir Matt gravely replied: 'Tut, tut, tut. I'm disappointed in you boys. Those other players have played twice as many games as you. Do you really think you deserve as big a bonus as them?'

They were forced to admit they were quite out of order. Exit two chastened young footballers with Sir Matt's final words ringing in their ears: 'Well, run along then and we'll say no more about it!' Mind you, Jimmy had a few more words to say to Fitzpatrick for the way he had put him in the firing line!

At the reunions of the Former United Players Association, guys in their seventies, like Johnny Carey, still call him Boss. He has held all his magnetism right through five decades. I remember in Rotterdam for the final of the European Cup Winners' Cup a lot of fans were gathered at the main entrance chanting the names of players like 'Hughesy' as they went in. Suddenly Sir Matt arrived and the rather wild cheering turned into respectful applause. It was quite touching, just like the Pope arriving. Matt is everybody's father. I remember the dinner that was held in honour of his 80th birthday. Cliff Morgan, the former Welsh Rugby Union star before becoming a big name with the BBC, was the speaker and there wasn't a dry eye in the house when he wound up a marvellous tribute to the grand old man of British football by saying, with no disrespect to his own dad: 'I wish I had had you as my father.'

You go through your life and meet maybe half a dozen truly educated people. One of my teachers told me that you meet plenty who are educated in one field but then you meet a Matt Busby, a great man with a roundness of spirit and education of life that makes him very special. I count myself very fortunate to have known him. He made the club and has left me an inheritance and obligation that makes me say to myself: 'I need to manage Manchester United in a very special way.'

He has set the benchmark of the institution. Of course, there has to be change but I know I must strive to maintain the core of dignity and class he created. He has thrown down the gauntlet and said: 'This is the way it should be done, this is Manchester United.' He is such a humble man as well, but then really great people usually have a humility without vanity.

I was reminded of what Matt created when I was at a match in the North East and a man pointed me out to his son and said: 'He is the manager of the greatest club in the world.' That's the legacy I have been left. Matt took a run-down club at the end of the last war and exploded Manchester United into a club of worldwide stature. When you are a bit down and things are not going right, as happens in football, it's encouraging to recall what the man in the North East said.

I cannot pay tribute to Sir Matt without acknowledging the debt Manchester United also owe to Jimmy Murphy. He was an extension of the manager, close to the players, particularly the youngsters and reserves he took under his wing to prepare for the first team. His contribution after the Munich air crash was such as to make you wonder if the club would have survived without him. Whenever I talked to him about the players who died in 1958, a tear would come into his eye. He was a lovely man. I think a part of him died, too, at Munich, but he was a doughty character and he pulled the club through. Though long retired, he scouted for me up until his sad death in November 1989. He and Sir Matt were different types but they complemented each other as many of football's famous partnerships have done.

Chapter Nine

PREMIER NONSENSE

The Premier League is a piece of nonsense. Its introduction this season has done the reputation of the clubs no good whatsoever and it has in fact alienated a great many supporters. I can imagine punters talking in the pubs and asking: 'What the hell is going on here, what's it all about, is there anything different about the new set-up except the fancy name?'

They still want us to play in the Zenith Cup in addition to the FA and Rumbelows Cup competitions of course, along with Europe if qualified. There are still the same 42 League games to be played and I understand that the international teams are due to play more fixtures.

So what price all the talk about streamlining the top division and aiming for quality rather than quantity? It would hardly behove the manager of a leading club to suggest that people both in and out of the game have been conned, but I can well understand the ordinary fan in the street wondering.

Hand in hand with the creation of the Premier League goes the television deal with BSkyB worth an impressive-sounding £304 million to football, but more accurately described in my view as a plain and simple rip-off. How the football people negotiating the contract did not have the savvy to know that once the agreement was signed the Sky people would fleece the fans, I will never know.

The agreement sells supporters right down the river and hits hardest at the most vulnerable part of society, the old people. At least ITV, with their more modest bid, were not bleeding the public dry.

Pensioners and thousands of people who can ill afford it must now buy a satellite dish to see top football on television, and then after the initial outlay they will have to pay £2.99 to watch the sports channel. I understand also that it is likely to go up to £6 a month before very long.

The Amstrad connection also worries me. There cannot be a supporter who does not view Tottenham's decision to vote for the Sky deal with a lot of suspicion. Even though the Spurs Chairman declared his interest as a boss of Amstrad, suppliers of the satellite dishes.

At the end of the day it seems to me that football is saying to the public, like it or lump it, please yourselves. Maybe that's the way of the world these days, but any decent organisation would have paid a bit more regard to the older supporters who have perhaps been actively watching for 50 years and spent fortunes travelling to see their team play before finally settling to watch football on television. Now they will have to pay through the nose for the privilege. What a kick in the teeth!

The fact that Rick Parry, the chief executive of the new League, and the high-flying Chairman Sir John Quinton couldn't figure out what would happen suggests to me that we have the wrong people running our game. I know Sky are putting a lot of money into football, but it's the fans who are paying the price and I don't like that. They pay enough already. If the television programme makers now think they own the game and that they can come dancing into training every day of the week for filming and interviews, they have another think coming. I will not be going out of my way to help them.

I couldn't believe the way the deal was done. Apart from the moral issue, did anyone really stop to think about the demands to follow and the damage to the game?

I am probably the only manager so far who has been forced to play two important Cup-ties on a Monday night a long way from home and it's very disruptive, as others will discover to their cost from now on. Two years ago we had to travel to play at Norwich and last season we were at Southampton. Faced with those kinds of journeys on a Monday a lot of supporters quite naturally stay at home, and those who come deserve medals.

You accept midweek replays as unavoidable, but to start off a tie on a Monday is diabolical. You need all the support you can get away from home at important Cup-ties, but of course that is hardly a consideration for the television people. All the traditional fervour of rival fans with their tammies and rikketies goes in a stroke despite the fact that that is the very essence of Cup football.

I know I have touched on this issue earlier, but it is important and I want to lodge my protest to at least try and prevent the situation from getting any worse. If I were to have a nightmare I'm sure it would feature an Orwellian scene of football being played entirely in some vast television studio without spectators, just people in their armchairs at home listening to canned cheers recorded in the dim and distant past at the Stretford End.

When we played at Norwich and Southampton we flew on the Monday morning to keep the disruption to a minimum, but you cannot ask supporters to fork out air fares. Those who still intend being there have to take at least half a day off work on Monday and probably need the next morning as well, either to travel or to recover from an all-night journey.

How much can you ask of supporters? I think the pattern before was acceptable. Nobody minded switching to a Sunday to accommodate ITV because it was still the weekend and acceptable to most people in return for the money coming into the game. You might have been watching sport on a Sunday afternoon anyway from the spectator point of view, and from the playing aspect playing one day later doesn't throw your whole system.

People are also usually free to travel on a Sunday, indeed the roads are often quieter, and if the match is played in the afternoon there is time to get back home in time to start the working week in the normal way. How fans are expected to make it to places like Norwich or Southampton, and vice versa of course, for Monday night football I don't know, except to say that the short answer is that they simply won't bother. That perhaps doesn't matter to television. After all, their concern is to keep people at home watching the box, but I suggest it matters very much to the game of football and it's time our leaders recognised it.

I know the proposal limits each club to two home matches on a Monday night, but this is meaningless because it doesn't take into account the number of times Manchester United will be asked to play away on a Monday. Sky only really want the top half dozen clubs on their screens, and once they have been to Old Trafford twice they will try to catch us playing away, and the same thing will happen with the likes of Arsenal and Liverpool. Home or away, it still adds up to playing Monday night football and as you will have gathered by now I consider it damaging to the game.

The whole business really disappoints me, and I wonder if Sky actually came out into the open during negotiations with the Premier League and explained the changes they intended making. That doesn't excuse the naïvety of our representatives who perhaps didn't look very far beyond the money on offer.

People accuse the big clubs of being greedy and running football for their own needs, but the people who put this deal through were the smaller clubs who weren't so much thinking of their supporters or the difficulty of preparing teams for Monday night football as aiming for a bigger slice of television money.

Six clubs voted against the Sky proposals and they were mostly the leading clubs, with the notable exception of Spurs. Manchester United were certainly opposed because we recognised the problems of playing on Monday nights which have implications far wider than difficult travel for the fans. For instance, Sky don't have as many viewers as ITV, and how are the club sponsors and advertisers going to feel about that? We also have an obligation to season ticket holders who buy their tickets on the assumption that they can watch traditional Saturday afternoon football. Will they want rebates now? A lot of United's support comes from other parts of the country, too. Monday nights won't be quite so convenient.

I can certainly see conflict ahead and I believe the game may come to rue the day we sold out to satellite television. I must hasten to add that there is nothing wrong with BSkyB itself. They are simply pursuing their own priorities and you can't blame them for striving for the best they can get after paying out £304 million. But what happens if Sky want to switch, say, Manchester United to a Monday night and we have a big European match on the Wednesday? It's hardly ideal

144

preparation, asking players to tumble out of bed following a tough night game to fly abroad in readiness for perhaps an even harder game just 48 hours later. Will Sky be understanding if the League fixture they want is a Championship decider? I wonder!

I have got to say also that Sky haven't got a commentary team to match the ITV line-up led by Brian Moore, who for me is the best. They haven't a former player of the calibre of Ian St John, even if he is so Liverpool biased he might as well wear an Anfield shirt, but that's another story. Sky still have a lot to learn. Take the game they covered between West Ham and Southampton. They kept Alan Shearer waiting out on the pitch at the end for nearly five minutes on a freezing cold night. Then they asked him a few silly questions until they finally got round to asking him the one they really had in mind: 'What's the truth about you going to Manchester United?' It was an impossible one for him to answer and he handled it well, simply replying that he was a Southampton player and had no idea of any transfer in the offing.

What have we let ourselves in for, I wonder? In my book it adds up to people paying more money for a poorer product. It's a mighty big change for football, and while we all have to stay flexible and adapt to a changing world, it doesn't mean you can disregard your fans and customers.

I can imagine quite a few Manchester United supporters will echo that sentiment and might suggest that I start applying the principle to my own club because Old Trafford is caught up in a sea of change at the moment.

The cost of watching football is increasing at all levels all over the country and I am afraid we have got caught up in the race to make sure we stay financially strong and so able to compete in the transfer market for the best players. I don't think the fans would forgive us if we let ourselves fall behind in the pricing structure so that we started to struggle for cash. Even Manchester United, the best supported club in the country, cannot compete with the top European clubs, who pay mind-boggling sums for the top players.

We cannot keep our best players as it is. Paul Gascoigne went to Lazio for over £5 million, despite a serious injury and operation, David Platt was transferred during the European Championships from Bari to Juventus for £8 million, while an Italian player, Gianluigi

Lentini, is reputed to have changed clubs from Torino to AC Milan for a package of some £30 million! Even our home-based transfers are fetching more and more with Alan Shearer moving from Southampton to Blackburn for £3.5 million.

At the same time I have got to say that I hope the United board stay mindful of the cost of watching football for the ordinary fan. I hope I shall never see the day when we price the traditional support out of the game and turn them into Sky armchair followers.

We have not been helped by the Justice Taylor Report which, following the inquiry into the Hillsborough disaster, decrees that First Division clubs must be all-seaters by season 1993-94. UEFA have taken the same safety line, so there is no escaping the need to have all our spectators sitting down. Again, personally I can't say I like it.

For one thing it means reducing the capacity of Old Trafford to around 44,000, which is about our average League attendance, so obviously for popular fixtures we are going to be turning people away – infuriating if you are a fan, and not very good business for the club.

But the real controversy centres on the Stretford End which this summer was pulled down and will be shut down for most of the season while a new all-seater stand is built, complete with cantilever roofing to complete the uniform line of the stadium.

Old Trafford will undoubtedly be the best soccer stadium in the country, and I include Wembley in that because while our big-game stadium is twice as large as Manchester United's ground, an alarming number of people have a very poor view of the pitch. Because of the wire fence protecting the pitch the spectators at the front tend to stand on their seats to see over the top. This means the people behind stand as well, and so on. I'm told it's chaotic, with stewards under fire with complaints and helpless to get people to sit down again ... and Wembley prices are certainly not cheap.

Old Trafford has already been designated as one of the four venues when the European Championships are staged in England in 1996. So we can be proud of our ground, though I am finding it difficult to visualise what it will look like at the Stretford End; and for all my arguments about the march of progress I cannot help but feel they will have torn the heart out of the ground. I tell myself that the Stretford End is only part of the structure and that the real heart of the club is the support, which won't die. Nevertheless, like a great many fans who have stood on the Stretford terraces down the years, I shall mourn its passing and the posh new stadium will look strange for a while.

The business of running the actual team won't change though, and we will follow our tried and tested routines. We have, for instance, a set preparation for a Saturday away game in, say, London, which I try not to vary. We travel on the Friday morning now to avoid getting caught up in the weekend rush and so that we can train when we get there to get the journey's stiffness and tightness out of the players' legs. Then on the morning of the match we all go for a loosening walk before an early light lunch with food like pasta. You have to watch some of the lads. If you let him, Steve Bruce would probably opt for a big steak with French fries and onions, followed by sago pudding. Unfortunately for him those days have gone. Meals for the modern professional footballer are planned to the last nutritional detail and for obvious reasons a good sleep in essential.

After the Friday evening meal, for instance, when they can eat virtually anything they choose, the players are not allowed to walk about the hotel. Other guests are naturally in a mood to relax and enjoy themselves and it is very tempting to invite a famous footballer into their company. It's not wise to be involved in that kind of environment before a match, so after perhaps a quick walk they are asked to keep to their rooms where they can watch television or perhaps gather for a game of cards.

I might add that we don't allow gambling at Manchester United, except for token stakes. They play games like Hearts, and someone would have to be very unlucky to lose £20 over the whole weekend. The gambling ban follows my experience as a player with Glasgow Rangers when it was not unknown for a player to lose thousands of pounds – hardly conducive to team spirit! There is something about the football fraternity that likes a gamble, but Rangers taught me a lesson and I won't have it at Old Trafford. To be fair, I think most clubs clamp down if they hear serious money is changing hands.

We have plenty of other fads to contend with, like superstitions, but these are harmless and I must confess that after a good result I try to stick to wearing more or less the same clothes for the next match.

147

Paul Ince likes to be the last on the pitch, still wriggling into his shirt as he runs down the tunnel. The last-minute routine varies for different players as well. For instance Neil Webb, Mike Phelan and Paul Ince don't go out for the pre-match warm-up. They prefer to do their stretches and loosening up in the dressing-room. I like to encourage the players to go out on to the pitch, but you have to take personal preferences into account as well, and at least I can see what they are doing in the dressing-room.

The ones who probably need watching are the lads on the field because there is this British habit of players simply wanting to shoot in at goal, and not bother with their exercises. That's kids' stuff, though, and I think we have educated them now into better habits. European players have always been much more meticulous, paying attention to their preparation, but I think we have caught up and are more professional about it these days.

I have my own routine as a manager of course. An hour before kick-off, after I have delivered my final team-talk, I like to get out of the dressing-room and away from the team. I think if you hover around right to the last moment you are conveying a lack of trust. A player has to take responsibility for his game once the whistle goes, and leaving him on his own for a while before the match helps him to face up to what lies ahead. It's a matter then of self-preparation and accepting the idea that he now has to stand on his own two feet. Once the referee blows his whistle, the manager, coach and physiotherapist are no longer in a position to help, so he might as well get used to it!

I do watch their faces, though, in the hours leading up to a game. They tell you a lot. Cocky players can suddenly go very quiet and it is interesting to see the mask slip from some of the loud ones. It helps you to understand their make-up when you are working in training during the week.

Everything that can possibly be done to help them is done and they are surrounded by capable experts who will range from the obvious people like the coach and physiotherapist to, say, the kit man. Norman Davies is the kit manager at Old Trafford and when we are away he and I go to the ground early. I take a look at the pitch while he lays out all the playing strips in our dressing-room. I once asked him why he didn't prepare a list of all the things he has to do, but he simply pointed to his head and said: 'It's all in there.'

Two or three clubs have a couple of kit men but we just have Norman. He does the lot, reserves and juniors included, and he works in conjunction with Norah and Sharon in our own laundry so that there is always clean gear every day for training and, of course, for matches. He is always on the ball, when it's just as easy to overlook something, as I recall from my Aberdeen days when we arrived for a match with the wrong set of shirts. I just can't envisage that happening at Old Trafford, although Norman is only human as we discovered when we played once at Luton following the death of Jimmy Murphy. We had been in touch with Luton, who had agreed to join us in a tribute to Jim by wearing black arm bands. I could hardly believe my eyes when the Luton players came out wearing theirs but our lads did not! Norman had forgotten to take them out of the hamper and we had to wait until half-time to put the matter right. It was very embarrassing and I guess Luton must have wondered about us. That was an isolated incident, though. He rarely forgets things and he's a character on the staff who helps create the right kind of happy atmosphere. Mind you, he is not the only character at Old Trafford.

I like to tell Jim McGregor that he's one sponge short of a full physio's kit. I hasten to add, that he is the best physiotherapist I've ever worked with. His knowledge is vast. He comes across larger than life at times, which is good at a football club. He does a lot more than treat injuries, important though this is, because he has the responsibility for meals and the movement of players to dovetail with training and matches. These are small but important details, a reflection of what we like to think is our thorough organisation. For instance, every day special meals are cooked for our young players at The Cliff training ground by two excellent cooks. I have an excellent back-up from people like Lynn, my secretary, and Kath on the switchboard, and at a club this busy you need that kind of support.

Our facilities, such as the treatment room and gymnasium for rehabilitation, are second to none, as you would expect from a club of this stature. In all, the Manchester United family provides an excellent working environment which would not be possible without the unstinting support of all members, both on and off the field.

149

But we must never allow ourselves to consider that we have reached the end of the road. In my quiet moments I am always thinking about how we can develop Manchester United in keeping with its great name. I came to Old Trafford with a vision for the future and the possibilities are truly exciting.

Our training base is at The Cliff in Salford but literally next door we have 18 acres at Littleton Road and I want to see this huge area developed into a massive training complex for youngsters. I believe that our whole system for schoolboys has to change.

At the moment professional clubs are allowed to give schoolboys coaching for one hour a week while the schools play them to the limit.

They play far too often in competitive matches for their age and physical capacity, and in my view would be far better off concentrating on the basic skills of the game with the kind of training a club like Manchester United is qualified to give.

I would like to see us develop our facilities so that we are in a position to coach young people every day and continue into the evenings under floodlights. This is the way forward to raise the standard of our young players.

Times have changed. All the great players of yesterday coached themselves by playing endless games in the street, perhaps with even a ball made of rags. Those days have gone. Lads expect much more these days and in any case the streets are full of cars. I think League clubs should take on the responsibility for bringing on these youngsters and offer them attractive facilities. We must keep this lifeblood coming into the game.

At Old Trafford we are paying more and more attention to the needs of our youngsters. We have for instance this summer appointed Paul McGuinness, son of Wilf, former United player and manager, to look after the educational needs of our trainees.

Paul has played professionally and he has been through Loughborough to qualify as a PE teacher so he knows the ropes and will help us to make sure we look after our young players both on and off the field. This is just one of the directions the club must travel if we are to progress.

I believe that we must also develop our medical responsibilities and I envisage a huge medical complex at our training ground which could be open for supporters and amateur players to use as well.

I am not short of ambition and my dream is to break new frontiers with Manchester United. If you stand still you in effect go back and I so very much want Manchester United in the forefront of football.

Chapter Ten

FERGUSON'S RED AND
WHITE ARMY

People talk about Manchester United trying to buy success and there is no disguising the fact that I have spent a lot of money in my six years as manager at Old Trafford. At the same time, I hope I have established that it is our dream to create our own players as well – a vision dating back to the Busby Babes and close to the hearts of all the club's followers. Just as Sir Matt found, though, you have to fill in key gaps by buying boldly and the facts are that up to the end of season 1991-92 I spent a total of £15.9 million on 21 players. The cost to the club has been offset by selling 26 to bring in £4.5 million.

This gives us a deficit of £11.4 million which averages out at an expenditure of around £2 million a year, a figure I believe in keeping for a club with the stature and resources of Manchester United. By today's prices, even £2 million does not necessarily guarantee you the purchase of one top player. I believe the fans who make us the best supported club in the country expect at least one new player every season so I am sure my financial strategy has been far from extravagant. I refute the idea that Alex Ferguson has spent fecklessly.

Hopefully, my transfer balance sheet will be changing yet again as this book goes to press and I look to the transfer market to improve our scoring rate which so let us down last season. For the record, I would like to give you the full list of my purchases and the fees:

Viv Anderson	(Arsenal)	£250,000
Brian McClair	(Celtic)	£850,000
Lee Sharpe	(Torquay)	£180,000
Mal Donaghy	(Luton)	£650,000
Jules Maiorana	(Histon)	£30,000
Paul Dalton	(Hartlepool)	£10,000
Jim Leighton	(Aberdeen)	£450,000
Mark Hughes	(Barcelona)	£1,600,000
Steve Bruce	(Norwich)	£800,000
Neil Whitworth	(Wigan)	£80,000
Neil Webb	(Nottingham Forest)	£1,500,000
Mike Phelan	(Norwich)	£750,000
Paul Ince	(West Ham)	£1,500,000
Gary Pallister	(Middlesbrough)	£2,300,000
Danny Wallace	(Southampton)	£1,200,000
Andy Rammell	(Atherstone Utd)	£25,000
Ralph Milne	(Bristol City)	£170,000
Denis Irwin	(Oldham)	£700,000
Paul Parker	(QPR)	£1,700,000
Peter Schmeichel	(Brondby)	£505,000
Andrei Kanchelskis	(Donetsk)	£650,000
	Total:	£15,900,000

All being well there will be another name or two to add to that list, as well as perhaps one or two departures as I shape the squad for an even more concerted effort for honours in the months ahead. Our biggest challenge, though, will be to learn from our mistakes of the past and resolve to try harder. Out of the disappointment of last season we will find a way. At times like this you draw on your character. Sometimes in adversity you become stronger. I know that I respond to a bad defeat quite positively and come up with answers more quickly and more clearly.

I remember at Aberdeen losing one of my early Cup finals 3-0 against Dundee United. The game was only three minutes old when I knew I had made a mistake and picked the wrong team. Looking back, I realised I had got caught up in a personal medical problem with one of the young players which had completely diverted my attention. The distraction cost me the Cup that season but I came to grips with my own role and recognised my error straightaway that night.

That experience, probably more than a lot of happier occasions, helped to forge my character in management terms. I suffered through the night but was up and running at eight the next morning. I was in at the ground first thing to wait for the players. I shook the hand of each one of them to say thank-you for getting the team to the Cup final. I told them there would be plenty of Cup finals in the future.

Character emerges when the chips are down and I think it all starts with your upbringing. If you study the background of people you can often get a true representation of them. Character is formed when you are young and is forged, to a great extent, by your parents. Take the religious bigotry you find in the world today. You look at families with bigotry in them and then examine their parents who are most likely to have had a similar outlook. I am proud and happy to say that I had wonderful parents who worked hard and passed on to me the value of that ethic. It's a personal sadness that my father did not live to see my successes. My mother died three weeks after my arrival in Manchester but at least she saw it all at Aberdeen and I know she was happy for me. I like to think that she approved of how both my brother and I turned out.

Like a lot of families in Glasgow ours was a mixed one from the religious point of view. My mother was a Catholic and my father a Protestant. As a result I came from a family with no regard for sectarian differences. I was the product of an environment in which hard work was appreciated. From time to time, I get a journalist asking to what do I owe my success. Far be it from me to analyse myself in terms of talent and ability and I always reply that the questions would be better asked of someone who knows me. I know deep down, though, that it has got to be the natural hard-working background I come from. If I was ever to pass on any advice it would be concentrated on the work ethic. It's as good a recipe for life as anything I know.

The area of Glasgow I came from was Govan, geographically and historically a peculiar place. It's at the very start of the city as the boats come in from the Irish Sea, so it was an obvious site for the shipbuilding which developed there. It had another peculiarity in that it was its own borough until the Second World War.

If you take a trip round the east and south of Glasgow those areas all come under the Govan school board. Most Govan people have their own identity, separate from Glasgow. I'm proud to let it be known I'm a Glaswegian but Govan has a special significance for me. As they say back home, you can take a boy out of Govan but you can't take Govan out of a boy.

That type of upbringing gives you a deep sense of belonging and at times you draw on it, particularly in adversity. There was not a lot of money flying about but my background was not poor because you never considered yourself poor. You had a pair of sandshoes and a football. The boots were hand-me-downs from perhaps a cousin and you didn't get those until you were 12. We never considered ourselves poverty-stricken, though, because there was always food on the table and you respected the hours your father put in at work.

There was a real sense of discipline about family life, even to the point towards tea-time when my mother would say to us children: 'Go and see if your dad is coming.' Dinner would go on the table when my dad walked in through the door and to get it right I had to watch out for him coming up the road. I would see all the workers teeming out of the yards, a sea of bonnets, because everyone wore caps in those days. I could pick out my dad half a mile away by the way he walked. I would sing out: 'He's at Harland and Wolf, now he's at the Plaza cinema.' I would chart his progress home through the well-known landmarks so that my mother produced the meal at just the right moment. My mother worked all her life on an industrial estate making aircraft parts. They were wonderful parents and created a solid platform for me.

As you get older you get passed on to someone else to look after you and I was fortunate to marry a woman who is absolutely 100 per cent for the family. It's Cathy's only real interest. Years ago, when I was a player, I would come home after a defeat expecting a little sympathy. I would be a bit depressed and quiet until Cathy would explode: 'Are you going to talk to these weans or not?' The importance of the family is immediately stressed and the humdrum would divert my thoughts away from the catastrophe of the Saturday afternoon.

There were more important things in life than football, at least as far as Cathy was concerned. I suppose she mostly brought up the kids and now I am very proud of our three children.

Mark, the eldest, has an honours degree in Chartered Surveying and has just gained his MBA in Paris. His life is at an exciting stage. He worked hard with his studies and he's ready to take to his wings which I hope will bring him satisfaction.

Jason is the mercurial member of the family. He has probably crammed more into his life already than both the others put together. He got his 'A' levels and then worked in Manchester for Granada Television. Then in mid-stream he quit work to go to Romania for four months to help care for the orphans. Everyone in the family was proud of the way he made the sacrifice. My reaction was that the task in Romania was for older people but Cathy thought it was a wonderful idea and I was treading on dangerous ground to oppose it. You don't want to encourage any more wrath than necessary!

My worry was that he had given up a good job but I realise now that, in later life, he will look back on that experience as part of his upbringing and will appreciate his backgound in the way I acknowledge mine prepared me for my life. Jason came back and is now working for BSkyB – at least he is until they read what I've had to say about them in this book! But he has ability and will do very well in television.

Then there is Darren, his twin but so different in temperament – they don't even look alike. Darren is the one keeping the family football flag flying. The only difficulty for me is that there could possibly come a time when I wish someone else could pick the team. Darren has a good talent, is a fine passer of the ball and if he could improve his goal-scoring he could distinguish himself as a midfield player. My concern is the problem of picking Darren if the team is losing or he has a bad game. Last season I started with him in the opening game but then he was injured and didn't play again in the League team until the very last match. So we haven't had to face any real test yet. It remains to be seen how the support takes to him. Someone told him that a few fans booed when his name was announced during the warm-up for one match. That worried me and the boy himself. We won't really know the reaction until he gets a run and I am faced with picking him after a poor performance.

There are certain players you select regardless of whether they have played well or badly. They are in on their long-term merits because you know their true level and what you will get from them most days. In the case of a fringe player it's a more difficult problem, especially if he is the manager's son. Bryan Robson and Paul Ince would play Darren all the time. They love playing alongside him. I just hope he is afforded the same opportunities as the rest and I hope I will be fair and not blinkered.

We have a great participation in all the kids' various interests and I have been fortunate in having such a good family. When I was in the valley of despondency few years ago and the football was not going right, the family was the anchor for me. The only problem was that last year Cathy definitely worried far too much about it all. She took too much on her shoulders and I must make sure she doesn't do that again. She has to be strong but I've told her to leave me to do the worrying.

As for myself, I am now 50 and, like a lot of people reaching that age, I went through a period of self-doubt. I wondered how many years I still had at the top and I must admit I was feeling terribly tired towards the end of last season. It probably tired everyone because to be involved in something so dramatic does drain you. I keep thinking back to Jock Stein literally dying at a match and my not paying him any attention. I saw him looking pale and perhaps not very well but I was so bloody wrapped up in a stupid game of football I didn't realise the man was critically ill and about to die.

Illness can creep up on us all. You read about Graeme Souness and his heart problem. You wonder whether it can happen to you. At the end of last season, I went for a full medical – treadmill, the lot. I'm happy to say the report has been good, quite encouraging – in fact, so good I might just pick myself for the team again!

The trick, of course, is not in years but in the contribution and one of my aims now is to seek inspiration from famous people. I've read some good books lately about the lives of characters like Armand Hammer, who was a millionaire by the time he was 21. Then there was Lew Grade, up at seven every morning, working a 12-hour day at the age of 85 and still apparently demanding so much from those around him. He is still looking for a perfect world like I'm looking for the perfect team. It's probably unattainable, but as we go into a new season I'm certainly looking for it, searching for a side capable of going through a whole season undefeated!

It's part of my make-up, the part which has contributed to the media continually annoying me by talking about 'Fergie Fury'. Certainly, I am driven by the need to succeed. I don't want failure and I find it hard to work with failure. So it is important, as we go into a new campaign, that I remind myself that we had a bloody good season last year. My job is perhaps different from the previous summer when I said we were setting out to win the League. The emphasis must shift and we must forget about winning the Championship because I know, now, that it will come anyway.

We are geared for it. We have got the club on the right footing. We have 67 players, ranging from juniors to seniors, and out of that 67, only 14 are over the age of 25. That gives you a good picture of the present day Manchester United. It's a young man's club and a grand football club again.

So far be it from me to look for a shoulder to cry on after last season's frustrations. I'm thinking in far more positive terms of how we can become better. I've passed the doubting stage in my life, wondering how long I can carry on. I'm over that and I know I have a good few years yet. I'm more concerned with the fact that, in my eyes, I've done nothing yet in terms of what really has to be achieved at this club ... winning the Championship.

We have rid ourselves of the paranoia when we got so uptight about everything. It was understandable because everyone was so aware of the prize. If you had seen the faces of the players after losing at Liverpool you would have realised that they appreciated it was much more than just another game of football. They were well aware of the need to play to the traditions of Sir Matt Busby. Sir Matt was heading for perfection with his Busby Babes who won the FA Youth Cup five years in a row. He had the football world at his feet when everything was so cruelly destroyed at Munich. Even that did not prevent him from starting all over again once he had recovered from his own grievous injuries. Our trials and tribulations of last season pale into insignificance. We have no excuse for not overcoming our dismay.

158

That's my vision for Manchester United. We are all ready to accept the challenge and, on a personal level, I am looking forward to doing battle again with my contemporary rivals like Howard Wilkinson, George Graham, Graeme Souness and Howard Kendall; and if along the way we have to annoy the old guy from Nottingham, so be it. We will always look on the bright side, as the fans sing so often. I feel more in control of the club. I am manager now, in the true sense of the word. I accept I have been on a learning curve, an apprenticeship if you like. I wish I could go back five years, knowing what I know now but I suppose most people would wish that about their jobs.

I think people appreciate more now what I'm trying to do. That's the message I'm getting when I hear the supporters chant: 'Ferguson's Red and White Army'. It gives me a feeling of immense pride and inspires me to achieve the vision Sir Matt Busby always had for Manchester United.